Excuse Me, Your Participle's Dangling!

How to Use Grammar to Make Your Writing Powers Soar

Catherine DePino

ROWMAN & LITTLEFIELD EDUCATION
A division of
ROWMAN & LITTLEFIELD PUBLISHERS, INC.
Lanham • New York • Toronto • Plymouth, UK

Published by Rowman & Littlefield Education
A division of Rowman & Littlefield Publishers, Inc.
A wholly owned subsidiary of The Rowman & Littlefield Publishing Group, Inc.
4501 Forbes Boulevard, Suite 200, Lanham, Maryland 20706
www.rowman.com

10 Thornbury Road, Plymouth PL6 7PP, United Kingdom

British Library Cataloguing in Publication Information Available

Library of Congress Cataloging-in-Publication Data Available

ISBN 978-1-4758-0276-4 (cloth : alk. paper) — ISBN 978-1-4758-0277-1 (pbk. : alk. paper) — ISBN 978-1-4758-0278-8 (electronic)

©™ The paper used in this publication meets the minimum requirements of American National Standard for Information Sciences Permanence of Paper for Printed Library Materials, ANSI/NISO Z39.48-1992.

Printed in the United States of America

To my husband and best friend, Dr. Andrew DePino:
outstanding teacher, department head, and actor

"Filled with moral virtue was his speech;
And gladly would he learn and gladly teach."
—Chaucer, *The Canterbury Tales*, general prologue

Contents

Preface

No matter what your circumstances, *Excuse Me, Your Participle's Dangling!* will give you the bare essentials of grammar that you'll need to write like a pro. This book also offers a simple yet foolproof method of writing under pressure, the key to success in any college program or workplace.

Will anyone care or even notice if your participles dangle or if you're stumped by which pronoun to use? Doesn't it sound right to say: "The lady at the spa gave my friend and *I* a make-over" rather than "The lady at the spa gave my friend and *me* a makeover"? Maybe, but is it good grammar? If you have to think about it for more than a second, this book's for you.

If you don't know the difference between a compound and a complex sentence, or if you can't tell when you've written a fragment or a run-on sentence, you're not alone. Why not hop aboard and learn grammar the easy way?

Are you getting ready for the demands of college writing? Shove this book in your backpack for a quick review before facing English placement tests, essay exams, and research papers. This book will definitely help if you're a college student who needs a no-hassle review of grammar and punctuation as it applies to writing.

Is English your second language? You need a guidebook with simple explanations that gives you just the right amount of grammar to write and speak with ease. This book will take you where you want to go with its student-friendly examples and self-quizzes.

Maybe you're a middle or high school teacher who needs a crash course in grammar basics before you begin to teach your class. It's been a long time since you've thought about the difference between action and linking verbs or have had to come up with a reason for using commas or semicolons in a sentence. But that's okay. This book is here to help refresh your memory and make you the best grammar/writing teacher you can be.

This book will bring it all back to you so that you can teach your students everything they need to know about grammar to realize their full potential as writers. Although I wrote this book for adults, *Excuse Me, Your Participle's Dangling* will give you many ideas that you can modify to suit your students' grade and ability levels.

Your students will find learning grammar fun if you can make it interesting by giving them some of your own humorous examples. More important, if you relate grammar directly to writing, your students will see the need for it and be more likely to want to learn it.

Are you a businessperson in any of the professions or trades (physician, CEO, salesperson, or plumber, for example) who has to depend on your secretary to proofread your work?

"I'm too busy," you say, but the truth is that you don't remember or you don't know where commas go, or how to tell the difference between *principal* and *principle*.

You've always wanted to know more about grammar and writing, but there wasn't time. You were too busy building your career, but now you're ready to learn. So what if the examples in this book sound sophomoric and take you back to sixth-period English with that nit-picking teacher who red-marked all your essays? You always said that high school was the best time of your life.

To sum it up, grammar is only a means to an end, a tool to help you write better. That's something your teacher probably never told you. It's not about the grammar. It's about the writing. By understanding grammar, you'll know how to express yourself beautifully in speaking and in writing.

Maybe your sentences are too fat, too skimpy, or you just can't think of anything to say when you write, especially under pressure. *Excuse Me, Your Participle's Dangling!* gives you a model for writing different types of sentences and shows you an efficient way to write when you're under the gun with essay exams or business reports.

You'll learn how to create a brief outline *before* writing and to proofread quickly and efficiently *after* writing so that your finished product will impress your reader. You'll also be able to dream up dynamite ideas when your professor or boss puts on the pressure. In short, you'll learn everything you need to know about grammar and writing without all the boredom and pain.

Acknowledgments

I'd like to thank Dr. Thomas Koerner, vice president and editorial director, and the best editor I've had in all my years of writing, for his advice and kindness. He knows the business better than anyone I know and takes a personal interest in all his projects.

Thanks also to Carlie Wall, a kind and helpful assistant editor and Carly Peterson, my conscientious production editor.

Thanks to my daughters, Melissa, Shayna, and Lauren, for your constant encouragement and love.

Introduction

How to Use This Book

This book is organized around questions many students ask when they learn grammar. I present the material in small bites, rather than big chunks, so that you can learn easily and effortlessly. Go through each chapter carefully, test yourself, and move on only after you grasp each concept.

When you see long lists of words (like the list of linking verbs in Chapter One), read them over a few times and remember why they're important. Don't bother memorizing them unless you have a lot of spare time on your hands. As long as you recognize certain words when you see them, you'll know enough to use them correctly. Otherwise, you'll find learning grammar a chore, and you want it to be a positive experience that will help you progress as a writer.

You'll also be more likely to persevere if you bring your own learning style to each lesson. You know best if you learn by seeing, hearing, or by doing hands-on activities. If you're a visual learner, who learns best by seeing, make up flash cards or charts; if you're an auditory learner, who learns best by hearing, tape the words and listen in; or if you're a kinesthetic learner, who needs hands-on activities to help you learn, make up little games and gimmicks to help you remember better.

You can also invent songs and raps or make lists to help you remember grammatical concepts that give you grief if you can't remember them any other way. Using the model sentences and punctuation you learn in this book to guide you, reinforce what you learn by dreaming up your own examples with your computer. Be creative. Whatever helps you learn is the most effective way for you to learn.

Take the quizzes, and check them against the answers in the back of the book. If you get a lot of answers wrong in a certain section, go back and review the chapter when you have time. Work at your own pace, and don't be afraid to make mistakes.

If you learn the information in one chapter each day, in less than two weeks, your writing will improve dramatically, and you'll gain confidence as a writer. You'll also learn shortcuts to help you with all the kinds of writing you'll do in college and on the job. Try all of them. They really work, and that's a promise.

And now, any questions?

Chapter One

Verbs

The Lifeblood of Sentences

When you start college, you'll begin your study of English in one of two places, a regular class or a remedial writing class sometimes dubbed "Bonehead English" or "English for Dummies" by grammar nerds. Frustrated students have to put out extra cash and don't get credit for sitting through what they should have learned in high school—all because they didn't pass an English grammar/composition placement test.

Where's the best place to begin to understand grammar? I've heard a lot about sentences, clauses, phrases, and pronoun agreement, and most of it boggles my mind.

If you take it one step at a time, you'll begin to understand the right amount of grammar you need to write well.

Once you understand verbs (called predicates when they're parts of a sentence) and subjects, you'll easily grasp all the other areas of grammar that will help you become a dynamic writer and speaker.

Whether your goal is to sidestep remedial English, to succeed in all your writing tasks in college or on the job as an employee or a boss, or to master English as a second language, let's begin by reviewing verbs, the lifeblood of sentences. Without action of some kind, you can't have a sentence. Verbs make your writing move. Nouns or subjects may be what your sentences are about, but verbs give them power and purpose.

1

TYPES OF VERBS

I never knew that verbs were so important. My teacher used to talk about action and linking verbs, and I tuned her out. What's the difference between the two?

It's simple. Action verbs express action: physical action, such as *drive, stomp*, or *bounce*, or mental action, such as *remember* and *believe*.

Some verbs, called *linking verbs*, or parts of the verb *to be,* don't express any action that's visible. Instead, they help form a complete thought by linking the subject (main idea) to some word in the sentence. The most common linking verbs are: *be* in all its forms (such as *am, are, is, was*, and *were*) and *feel, grow, look, remain, smell, sound*, and *taste.*

Remember that linking verbs don't show action. Instead, a linking verb indicates a state of being or existence. It tells you something's happening, but you can't see the action. A linking verb means you're there. You exist—even if you're sprawled out on your bed watching a sitcom.

Be cautious because some linking verbs can masquerade as action verbs, depending on how they're used in sentences. Generally, you can call a verb *linking* if you can replace the verb with *is* or *was.*

Let's look at a couple of sentences to see if you can determine if the verbs used are action or linking verbs. In this sentence would you call *smelled* a linking or an action verb?

The gym locker *smelled* so horrible that Coach Gung Ho decided to call in sick.

In this sentence the verb *smelled* is used as a linking verb because you can't see the gym locker actively doing anything although you can probably picture Coach holding his nose, tearing out of the gym, and bellowing, "I'm out of here."

Smelled functions as a linking verb in this sentence because it expresses the state of the gym locker room rather than an *action* someone's performing. You can also substitute the verb *was* for *smelled* in this sentence—more proof that *smelled is* a linking verb.

Here's another sentence with the verb *smelled:* Do you think it's used as a linking verb or an action verb?

When Tiara *smelled* the rotten flounder, she threw it down the garbage disposal and sprayed her kitchen with air freshener.

Even if you're a person whose participles dangle, you probably said that *smelled* is used as an action verb in this sentence. You know this because you can visualize Tiara sniffing the bad flounder, tossing it in the disposal, and dancing around the room with the air freshener. There's definite action going on in this sentence. Also, you can't substitute *is* or *was* for *smelled* in this sentence.

Let's examine another sentence. The verb *looked* can also be an action or a linking verb. How do you think it's used in this sentence?

Monique's pet basset hound *looked* snappy dressed as Count Dracula in a black cape and bow tie for the costume party.

In this sentence you can substitute *was* for *looked,* so *looked* is a linking verb. Remember that this little trick will help you tell whether a verb is an action verb or a linking verb. *Was* fits in this sentence as easily as the verb *looked.*

You can see in this sentence that the linking verb *looked* doesn't show action. Instead, this linking verb shows a state of being or existence. In this sentence *looked* is more about the basset hound's state and how he appeared, rather than about anything he did.

Think about the verb *looked* in the next sentence. Is it used the same way or differently from the way it's used in the previous example?

Dante *looked* out the window in shock as a purple, bald man with claws emerged from a spaceship.

Did I hear you say action verb? Give yourself an *A*. You know that *looked* is an action verb because you can visualize Dante peering out the window at the purple, bald man, and saying, "Is it reality, or is it the tequila I imbibed at that party last night?"

Also, if you substitute the word *was* for the word *looked* in this sentence, you know it wouldn't make sense.

Why do grammar gurus say not to use a lot of linking verbs in writing?

Whenever you can, use action verbs. They breathe life into your sentences and rivet your reader to the page. When you use linking verbs too often, your writing falls flat and lacks energy. Sometimes you have to use linking verbs, but don't use them all the time.

Here's an example of a sentence using a linking verb:

Some people in my aerobics class *were* so talkative that we couldn't hear the instructor.

Were is the linking verb because it's part of the verb *to be*. If you don't want to use a linking verb in this sentence, you can substitute *talked*, an action verb:

Some people in my aerobics class *talked* so much that we couldn't hear the teacher.

Which sentence do you prefer?
   I like the second example best. It's more direct and shows the action better.

Not to change the subject (although you may need a break by now), but throughout this book you'll find a quick quiz to help you assess your understanding of each lesson.

Give yourself a reasonable amount of time—a minute or two for each question. Put your score at the top of each quiz and circle it, or you can write the number you got correct over the number of questions at the top of your paper.

Your score will give you an idea of how much more you need to study to master each concept you learn. If you get more than two wrong, go back and review the section that gave you trouble until you think you understand it thoroughly.

QUICK QUIZ #1: ACTION VERB OR LINKING VERB?

In the space at the end of the line, write whether you think the bold print verbs are used as action (A) or linking (L) verbs. You can find the answers to this quiz in the back of the book under Quick Quiz #1.

1. I **felt** that my brain went into slow gear after my teacher's lecture on transitive verbs. _____
2. Tasha **tasted** the white chocolate spiders, but she said she preferred milk chocolate cashews. _____
3. The hairy troll **appeared** on stage, ran out to the audience, and asked Hortense to marry him. _____
4. The casserole **tasted** delicious until Len discovered that it contained snails and eels. _____
5. When Antoine would not wake up for school, his mother **sounded** a loud alarm to rouse him. _____
6. The tomato plants that Dylan **grew** won him top prize in the gardening contest. _____

7. Clay's excuse for not doing his math homework **sounded** unbelievable, so his teacher assigned him double problems the next night. _____

8. When Bongo, my cat, **smelled** the salmon, she did flips in the air. _____

9. When Andrew **felt** his horse's heartbeat with a stethoscope, he knew his pet would survive and thrive. _____

10. Ms. Ramirez **grew** weary of explaining linking verbs, so she said, "Let's have a popcorn party instead." _____

STRONG VERBS TRUMP WEAK VERBS

In addition to avoiding linking verbs, you'll also want to steer clear of weak action verbs if you're aiming to dazzle readers with your writing. Weak verbs show up in sentences as lifeless, lackluster verbs that don't describe the action in a vibrant, colorful way.

You can tell they're weak because you can't picture the action. Picture the colors gray, brown, or beige versus turquoise, magenta, or canary yellow. Strong verbs, like these flaming colors, reach out and grab you, luring readers on to read more of what you wrote. Sure, grays, browns, and beiges, like linking and weaker verbs, will work once in a while, but most of the time, you'll want to make your verbs shout out your writing presence as bright colors do.

Whenever you can, add zing to your verbs. You can do this by picturing the action in your sentence and finding the best word to describe it. Hunt for the perfect action word. Make your reader visualize the action as if it's happening in real time.

Here are some examples of how using strong verbs rather than weak verbs can spice up your sentences. Notice how you can picture the strong verb in each example.

Weak Verbs: The silver stallion *rode* into the magenta sunset.

Strong Verbs: The silver stallion *galloped* into the magenta sunset. (You'll see the action more clearly here because of the strong verb.)

Weak Verbs: The cat *ate* part of the hairy spider and *left* it at my feet.

Strong Verbs: The cat *devoured* the hairy spider and *dropped* it at my feet.

Weak Verbs: Grandma *worked* the pizza dough and *threw* it in the air.

Strong Verbs: Grandma *pummeled* the pizza dough and *twirled* it in the air.

ACTIVE VOICE VERSUS PASSIVE VOICE

Do you want another way to rev up your writing so that your reader can feel the full impact of your message? Try using active voice rather than passive voice whenever you can. Active voice is exactly what it implies. When you use it, it activates and jump-starts your sentence instead of dragging it down with the weight of a linking verb followed by the past participle of a verb. If you're wondering why it will help you to know about past participles, let me explain.

Before learning about the passive voice, we'll need to learn about past participles because passive voice contains a form of the verb *to be* or linking verb and the past participle of a verb. Later, we'll look at some examples and see how active voice makes your writing sizzle rather than drag.

Don't let the term *past particle* intimidate you. A participle is simply an action word that ends in one of these endings: *ing (hoping); d (amazed); ed (smashed); n (broken); en (fallen);* and *t (spent)*. We call these words past or present participles because their endings let us know the action happened in the past or is happening now.

Most of the time, past participles end in *d* or *ed*. You'll see in the examples below how the past participle is paired with the helping verb *have* or another form of it, such as *had*. Note that the present participle is the *ing* form of a verb, as in *talking, hollering,* and *dancing*.

IRREGULAR VERBS

The tricky part comes into play when you find out that some verbs are irregular in that they don't follow any predictable pattern in forming the past and past participles. Regular verbs are predictable in that they end in *d* or *ed*. We call verbs like *sing, bring,* and *drink* irregular verbs because you don't form their past and past participles by adding *d* or *ed* the way you do with regular verbs.

Later in the book, I'll show you how you can use participles to describe nouns and verbs in a sentence. You'll also learn how to avoid dangling participles so that you'll never stand accused of this glaring error.

To put it simply, every verb has four principal parts: present (the verb in its raw form), past, past participle, and present participle. You can easily figure out the principal parts of most verbs. You've probably come across the present part of the verb (sometimes called the *infinitive*, which is used with *to*) when you studied another language.

You'll find it easy to learn the parts of regular verbs. The best way to learn the parts of irregular verbs is to study the list below. Of course, there are many more regular and irregular verbs that you can easily find online if you're interested.

Table 1.1 Examples: Principal Parts of Regular Verbs

Present	Past	Past Participle	Present Participle
achieve	achieved	have achieved	achieving
bake	baked	have baked	baking
burp	burped	have burped	burping
call	called	have called	calling
kiss	kissed	have kissed	kissing
rush	rushed	have rushed	rushing
smile	smiled	have smiled	smiling
tumble	tumbled	have tumbled	tumbling

Here are some irregular verbs than often cause people trouble. Can you think of any others?

Table 1.2 Examples: Principal Parts of Irregular Verbs

Present	Past	Past Participle	Present Participle
burst	burst	have burst	bursting
do	did	have done	doing
eat	ate	have eaten	eating
go	went	have gone	going
ring	rang	have rung	ringing
shrink	shrank	have shrunk	shrinking
steal	stole	have stolen	stealing
swim	swam	have swum	swimming
write	wrote	have written	writing

As you look over the past participles of irregular verbs, it may remind you of how some children learning the language make up their own versions of the past tense or past participles of irregular verbs.

In forming the past tense and past participles, they're probably trying to follow the pattern for regular verbs. But as you've seen, sometimes grammar doesn't follow a logical pattern. Maybe you've heard a small (or not so small) child say, "I seed [or seen] the horse jump over the fence"; "Boohoo, my balloon bursted"; or "I have swimmed in my pool all summer."

It's easy to make mistakes with irregular verbs; that's why it's helpful to look over this list and to find more examples to help you avoid causing eyebrows to raise by saying, "I've already wrote the report," when your boss asks what happened to the memo you were supposed to have *written*.

Now that you've learned about past participles, here's an example of passive voice, that clunky construction consisting of part of the verb *to be,* and sometimes using the helping verbs *has, have,* or *had,* plus the past (*ing* form) participle of a verb.

Passive Voice: Leftover liver and onions *was served* by the CEO at the new employees' reception. (In this sentence you see *was*, part of the verb *to be,* followed by the past participle of *serve*.)

Here's how the sentence sounds when we change it to active voice:

Active Voice: The CEO served leftover liver and onions at the new employees' reception. (We changed the passive voice to active by moving the subject of the sentence, *CEO*, to the forefront and using the past tense of the verb *serve* instead of the verb *to be* (*was*) plus the past participle of *serve*.)

Here's another example of passive and active voice. You be the judge of which sounds livelier and less awkward.

Passive Voice: The horse's incessant whinnying was heard by all the farmer's neighbors. (Note that the verb *was heard* is in passive voice.)

Active Voice: All the farmer's neighbors heard his horse's incessant whinnying. (*Neighbors* is the subject, and the verb *heard* is in past tense rather than the past participle form used in the previous sentence.)

Why do you think the active voice delivers the message better in this sentence?

It doesn't use as many words (nine words versus eleven) to get the same idea across, and it's more to the point than the other sentence. It just sounds better to me.

Right answer! Do you have any other questions about passive voice?

Here's one: Is it ever okay to use passive voice?

Actually, sometimes it is. Maybe you have a situation in which you can't or don't want to identify the person who performs an action:

When I said there would be no questions asked about who pilfered it, my salami and cheese sandwich was returned to my backpack.

You may also want to use passive voice when you don't know who is performing the action in a sentence, as in:

An anonymous love letter was sent to my friend Marsha.

If you're writing a research paper or a report for your business, you'll occasionally want to use linking verbs because technical topics might require a more formal tone. That's perfectly understandable. Just make sure that the bulk of your writing sparkles with strong, active verbs.

Example: No evidence of stomach upset *was seen* in those who were given the sugar pills.

QUICK QUIZ #2: ACTIVE OR PASSIVE VOICE?

Now it's time to take a quiz on active and passive voice. Write whether the italicized verbs are written in active or passive voice. Write A for active voice and P for passive voice. Score 10 points for each correct answer. Find answers in the back of the book under Quick Quiz #2.

1. So many memos *were sent* by the boss that Blair ignored them until he got one saying, "You're fired." _____
2. Dr. Arbitrary *calculated* our grades by letting his dog sniff our essay tests: if Wolf barked, we got an A; if he growled, we got a D. _____
3. The rolls that *were baked* in our company cafeteria tasted dry and salty. _____
4. The mushy shepherd's pie that the banquet staff *served* motivated us to start a Zumba class and dance during our lunch hour. _____
5. Bindi's blind date *impressed* her by arriving at her apartment in a limo, carrying a pound of premium candies and a bouquet of daffodils. _____
6. The supervisor *was annoyed* that Zara constantly texted her boyfriend during work hours. _____

7. Tory *ran* when he saw the hungry bull moose charge toward him at the campsite. _____

8. The waitress *confused* our order and gave us burgers and fries instead of steak and au gratin potatoes. _____

9. When calories *are being counted*, it doesn't help when someone presents you with strawberry shortcake oozing with whipped cream. _____

10. Mai *opened* the door in her moth-eaten pajamas and muddy face-mask, and her friends shouted, "Surprise. It's party time!" _____

Chapter Two

How to Build a Sentence
from Start to Finish

Now that I can recognize a verb anywhere, even a linking verb, show me an easy way to find the subject of a sentence.

After you find the verb (called *predicate* when it's part of a sentence), you'll have no problem finding the subject of the sentence—*who* or *what* the sentence is about. To find the subject, simply ask *who* or *what* before the predicate. You need both a subject and a predicate to build sentences.

Example: The hungry squirrel nibbled the walnut.

(verb: *nibble,* an action verb) If you ask who nibbled the walnut, you'll get the answer, the *squirrel.* The subject of the sentence is squirrel. *The* and *hungry* are adjectives, which modify (tell us something about) the squirrel.

Check out these two sentences, one with a linking verb and another with an action verb. See if you can find the subjects.

Example 1: The wonton soup tastes salty.

You know that *tastes* is a linking verb because it doesn't show any action you can see. Instead, it states a characteristic of the soup. When we ask *what* tastes salty, we get the answer *soup.* *The* and *wonton* are two adjectives modifying soup.

Remember that in some cases, *taste* can show up as an action verb, as in:

***Taste* this savory pasta fagioli that simmered for hours.**

If you ask *who* or *what* in front of the linking verb *tastes* in this sentence, you'll find that *you* is the subject even though we can't see it. When we study independent clauses, you'll learn more about *you*, which can sometimes show up as an invisible subject.

Example 2: Grammar is exciting.

In this sentence *is*, a linking verb, is the predicate, and *grammar* is the subject.

Is finding the subject always that simple?
    Sometimes you have to think a little to find the subject, but it's still easy. Here's a sentence to think about:

The woman in the office next to mine eats jelly worms all day.

What do you think is the subject of this sentence?
    The action word or predicate is *eats*, and if I ask *who eats*, I get the answer *woman*. I'd say that *woman* is the subject. But what do you call those other words between the subject and the predicate?
    Yes, *woman* is the subject. Those other words, *in the office next to mine*, are two prepositional phrases that describe *woman*. But we'll talk more about them later. For now, if you ask the question: *Who eats jelly worms*, the only logical answer is *woman*. You know it can't be *office*, *mine*, or any of the other words in the sentence.

QUICK QUIZ #3: SUBJECTS AND PREDICATES

Here's a quick quiz on subjects and predicates, the two parts of speech crucial to every sentence. Read the sentences below and name the subjects (S) and predicates (P) in the spaces at the end of the line. Score 10 points for each correct answer (each sentence contains 20 points), for a total of 100 points.

1. The sophisticated cat ate only lobster and filet mignon.
        S _____ P _____
2. The walrus waddled over to the zookeeper.
        S _____ P _____
3. The basketball player in the red jersey dunked the ball every time.
        S _____ P _____

4. My canary existed on a diet of frog's legs and water chestnuts.

     S _____ P _____

5. The man in the chartreuse jacket is my English professor.

     S _____ P _____

DIRECT AND INDIRECT OBJECTS

I'd like to know how to find the object of the sentence. And while you're at it, please explain the difference between a direct and an indirect object.

It's easy to find the direct object of a sentence. All you need to do is ask *whom* or *what* after the action word (predicate). Some sentences have direct objects, but others don't. To see if you do have a direct object, simply reverse the process of asking *who* or *what* in front of the verb that you used to find the subject.

Here's an example:

Liam found his schnauzer on the beach. (Liam found whom or what? The direct object of the sentence is *schnauzer*.)

With indirect objects you have to stick an extra word in your question to get the answer. You have to ask *to* or *for whom or what* after the verb. Look at these examples:

Natasha gave her brother a stinkbug for his bug collection.

Natasha gave whom or what? When we ask *Natasha gave what*, we get the answer, *stinkbug*, which is the direct object. However, to find the indirect object we need to ask *to* or *for whom* or *what*. In this sentence, we ask: Natasha gave *to whom*, and we come up with the answer, *brother*.

Here's another example of a sentence with both a direct and an indirect object:

The job applicant sent the employer a ten-page résumé listing all her accomplishments from grade school to graduate school.

The direct object is *résumé*. We asked *sent what* to get the answer *résumé*. The indirect object is *employer*. We need to ask *sent to whom?* to come up with that answer.

You've mastered subjects and predicates as necessary parts of all sentences, and you've learned about direct and indirect objects. Now we'll turn to clauses, the building blocks of sentences.

Why do I need to know about clauses? That was the most boring part of grammar and something I never understood.

Knowing about independent and dependent (sometimes called main and subordinate) clauses will help you learn to write the four different types of sentences: simple, compound, complex, and compound-complex. Once you can identify each sentence type, you'll be able to vary them, mix them, and match them to wow your teachers or employers with writing that will make them beg for more.

Possibly the best benefit from knowing about clauses and sentence types will come when you can pinpoint your own errors in sentence structure. Knowing about the two types of clauses will alert you to two of the biggest writing blunders, run-on sentences and sentence fragments.

Isn't it reassuring to know that you have to learn about only *two* types of clauses and *four* types of sentences to help you produce your best writing? As a bonus, you'll also find it easier to master punctuation. Knowing about clauses will also help you develop your own writing style and help you write quickly and efficiently when you're under pressure.

I usually guess at punctuation. How can learning different sentence types help me punctuate better?

If you understand independent and dependent clauses, you'll better understand when to pause and when to speed up when you read a sentence.

Some teachers say that you should read a sentence aloud and insert a punctuation mark when there's a pause or when the inflection (change in the pitch or tone) of your voice varies. But that doesn't always work because not everyone reads with perfect expression, knowing exactly when to pause or when to keep reading. Learning about clauses will give you definite guidelines to use when you're not sure about punctuation.

Here are two examples of how knowing about clauses can give you clues about commas. Which sentence needs commas, and where would you put them? Try reading the sentences, and think about where you would pause or not pause.

1. **Employees who left work early were served tuna surprise in the company café.**
2. **Duncan Dweeb who left work early was served tuna surprise in the company café.**

If you said that sentence #2 needs commas after *Dweeb* and *early*, give yourself a star. The fact that the first sentence doesn't have commas shows us that the employees who left work early were the only ones who got the tuna surprise.

In sentence #2, the basic meaning of the sentence is that Duncan Dweeb was served tuna surprise in the company café. The fact that he left work early is additional information in this sentence. We set it off with commas to show that it's added information.

Did you notice that you probably didn't pause when you read the first sentence but that you did pause when you read the second one? If you aren't sure about when to pause when reading these sentences, knowing about clauses will help you pinpoint the right answer.

THE INDEPENDENT CLAUSE

I'm ready to learn about clauses now—but spare me the dreary details.

I'll make it as painless as possible, and you may even enjoy it because of the benefits it will bring you. Now that you've learned about subjects and predicates, mastering clauses will be easy. Let's start with the independent clause. Think about what it means to be independent. When you're independent, you can succeed without anyone's help. You don't need anyone to hand you a bag of groceries or a stash of cash to pay the rent. Independent clauses are like that too. Basically, an independent clause is a simple sentence that can stand alone and make good sense.

Here's an example: **The hefty hippopotamus flopped from the high dive into the pool.**

It's easy to see that *flopped* is a verb because it shows action. We can visualize the hippo flopping in the pool and making a loud splash. When we ask the question, "Who flopped?" we get the answer *hippopotamus*. *The* and *hefty* are adjectives describing the hippo.

This sentence is a simple sentence because it has a subject, *hippopotamus*, and a predicate, *flopped*. More importantly, it expresses a complete thought.

Now here's a brainteaser for you. The following one word is a sentence. Can you explain why?

WIGGLE.

You must be kidding. I don't see any subject. There's only a predicate. How can it be a sentence?

Look at the sentence again and ask yourself *who* wiggles. The subject, of course, is *you*, but the *you* is understood rather than stated. Whenever you see a sentence giving a command, the subject is always *you,* and it's definitely a sentence. Even though it's invisible, it's there working behind the scenes as the subject of a sentence.

To recap: If you want to determine if you've written an independent clause (simple sentence), ask yourself what the predicate (action word) is. Once you know that, ask *who* or *what* in front of the predicate. Then you can identify the subject. If the group of words makes sense—presto, you've created an independent clause (simple sentence).

DIFFERENT TYPES OF SENTENCES

My English teacher once complained that I use too many simple sentences. Why is this a problem?

Teachers sometimes caution against using too many simple sentences. They have a point because a lot of simple sentences can make your essays look childish and skimpy, like elementary school writing. But sometimes using a simple sentence at the beginning or at the end of your paper can make an important point leap out at your reader and command attention.

You can also throw a simple sentence in the middle of your paper to change the pace of your writing. When you fear that your boss might break into a pig-snout snore while reading your sales report, a simple sentence can break the monotony, jolting the drowsy head honcho awake.

You may have noticed that authors sometimes use simple sentences to create special effects. Poe's "The Tell-Tale Heart" is the perfect example. The narrator speaks in short, staccato sentences to show us his disturbed mental state.

After you're able to identify different types of sentences, you can make your sentences fit the mood you're trying to evoke when you write a report, essay, or story. Slow down the pace with longer sentences, and pick it up with short, snappy sentences.

Now that you've reviewed subject and predicate and learned how to identify an independent clause (simple sentence), it's time to build upon the simple sentence to create compound, complex, and compound-complex sentences. Then you'll know how to write an endless variety of sentences, and everyone will sing your praises and call you a grammar genius.

What's another type of sentence I can use to give my writing more variety?

A compound sentence is another type of sentence that will help you vary your writing style. You already know that a simple sentence is made up of one independent clause. A compound sentence has two or more independent clauses. To write a compound sentence, take two independent clauses (simple sentences), add a conjunction, and magically meld them into one sentence. Here's an example:

Two Simple Sentences:

1. **Juan ate caviar at the party. (independent clause)**
2. **You could also call it pickled roe of sturgeon (fish eggs). (independent clause).**

Compound Sentence (two independent clauses joined by *but*):

Juan ate caviar at the party, but you could also call it pickled roe of sturgeon (fish eggs).

In this compound sentence there are two independent clauses with two separate subjects (*Juan, you*) and two separate predicates (*ate, call*). Also notice that the two independent clauses are joined by *but*, which we call a *coordinating conjunction.*

The other coordinating conjunctions are: *and, for, or, nor, yet,* and *so.* However, we use *and* and *but* more often than the others. Our sample sentence is compound because we've combined two independent clauses or two simple sentences, joining them with a conjunction.

Would it matter if we used *and* instead of *but* in the last sentence example?

It sounds better to use *but* in this sentence because this conjunction introduces a contradictory thought or an element of surprise (finding out that caviar was fish eggs).

Whenever you choose words, even little ones like *and* or *but*, think of the impact they'll have on your reader. Your reader will tune in more easily and know exactly what you mean if you take the time to consider the shades of meaning in words.

My teacher said that not all sentences with *and* or *but* are compound. Please explain.

Your teacher was right. Look at this sentence:

The frisky frog kissed Katie's hand and left three lumpy, bumpy warts on her fingers.

If you think this sentence is compound, read it again. Does it have two *separate subjects* and two *separate predicates*?

Look at the sentence closely, and you'll see that it's a simple sentence with a compound predicate (*kissed* and *left*). Notice that there isn't a second subject after *and.*

When you ask *who* left the lumpy, bumpy warts on Katie's fingers, you won't come up with an answer because there isn't any. But, of course, we all know who did it because the subject of the independent clause tells us it's the frog.

In other words, each group of words joined by the conjunction must have a separate subject and a separate predicate to make the sentence compound. An easy way to test this is to ask yourself if each group of words could stand on its own as two separate sentences if you eliminated the conjunction. In this case, only the first group of words could stand alone and make sense.

To make the sentence compound, simply add a subject to the second group of words:

The frisky frog kissed Katie's hand, and *it* left three lumpy, bumpy warts on her fingers.

What more do I have to know before I can write a complex sentence, the next sentence type you mentioned?

Don't be put off by the word *complex.* There's nothing difficult about it. Learning this type of sentence will add depth and texture to your writing and will make you look like a writing wizard. To write a complex sentence, all you have to do is compose an independent clause (a clause that can stand alone) and add one or more dependent clauses.

We call them dependent clauses (or subordinate clauses) because they need to latch on to other words to make sense. Alone they'd be miserable.

To give you an idea of how to create different sentence types to enliven your writing, let's look at a simple sentence transformed into a compound sentence. Then you'll see how easy it is to give the compound sentence a makeover to change it into a complex sentence.

Simple Sentence: James asked Kia to the concert.

Compound Sentence: James asked Kia to the concert, but she didn't want to date boring guys.

Complex Sentence: When James asked Kia to the concert, she told him that she didn't date boring guys who wore pocket protectors and carried attaché cases.

As you can see, the *simple* sentence contains one complete thought (independent clause). The *compound* sentence adds a second independent clause, linking it with the conjunction *but*. Finally, the complex sentence contains an independent clause (*she told him*) and three dependent clauses (*When James asked Kia to the concert, that she didn't date boring guys*, and *who wore pocket protectors and carried attaché cases*).

THE DEPENDENT CLAUSE

Tell me more about dependent clauses.

Like an independent clause, a dependent clause has a subject and a predicate—but with one important difference. Can you tell what it is?

I can see that a dependent clause (for example, *When James asked Kia to the concert*) doesn't make sense and can't stand alone. But how else can I tell a dependent clause from an independent clause?

In addition to what you said, a dependent clause contains certain words that act like red flags to signal its beginning. There are two kinds of words that let you know a dependent clause is coming up. The first group is called *subordinating conjunctions*.

Here's a list of subordinating conjunctions: *after, although, as, as if, as long as, as though, because, before, if, since, so, so that, that, though, till, unless, until, when, whenever, where*, and *while*.

THE DIFFERENCE BETWEEN CLAUSES AND PHRASES

I wasn't a grammar whiz, but I vaguely remember my teacher saying that some of those subordinating conjunctions can also be called prepositions.

Yes, sometimes the same words are used as prepositions, but don't let that confuse you. It all depends on how they're used in a sentence.

You may remember from past English classes that a prepositional phrase starts with a preposition and ends with a noun or pronoun. Since we're going to discuss phrases throughout this book, you'll want a short definition. *A phrase is simply a group of words without a subject and a predicate that you can use as a single part of speech, such as an adjective or an adverb.*

Unlike a clause, a prepositional phrase doesn't have a subject and a predicate. It has a preposition, possibly some adjectives, and an object of the proposition. Later on we'll review prepositions and look at more examples of prepositional phrases. For now, it's enough to know the difference between a prepositional phrase and a dependent clause.

Here are two examples of a phrase and a dependent clause using *after*, which could be either a subordinating conjunction or a preposition, depending on how it's used.

Compare these sentences and see if you can tell the difference between the dependent clause and the prepositional phrase.

1. *After the play* **we went to Daren's house and ate roast beef and horseradish sandwiches.**
2. *After we saw the play,* **we went to Daren's house and we ate roast beef and horseradish sandwiches.**

I'd say the first sentence starts with the prepositional phrase and the second starts with the dependent clause.

Good! How did you decide which was the phrase and which was the clause?

Easy—the phrase starts with *after* (used as a preposition) and ends with a noun. The dependent clause starts with *after* (used as a subordinating conjunction) and has a subject, *we*, and a predicate, *saw*.

You've got it! Do you have any more questions about clauses?

You mentioned a second group of words that signal a dependent clause. What are these words called?

Relative pronouns can also signal a dependent clause. And this will make you happy—you only have to remember a few relative pronouns: *who, whose, whom, which,* and *that.*

Look at this sentence using *who* as a dependent clause opener: **The teacher *who accused me of dangling my participles* is now eating her words.** Why do you think the italicized clause is a dependent clause?

From what I can figure, it starts with *who*, a relative pronoun, and it can't stand by itself.

Bravo! Now, by process of elimination, what is the independent clause in the sentence?

That's easy—*The teacher is now eating her words.*

Excellent! Now here's something to challenge your brain: Did you notice anything different about the dependent clause in this sentence compared to the one that started with the subordinating conjunction?

Yes, come to think of it. I see that the word *who*, which starts the dependent clause, seems to be the subject of the dependent clause. The dependent clause doesn't have a separate subject.

And that's okay. In some complex sentences, the relative pronoun wears two hats. It's both the dependent clause opener *and* the subject of the dependent clause.

I'm a little confused. You said that an independent clause could stand alone and expresses a complete thought. I'm wondering if *she told him* **in the sentence about James asking Kia to the concert makes sense by itself. Here's the whole sentence:** *When James asked Kia to the concert, she told him that she didn't date boring guys who wore pocket protectors and carried attaché cases.* **Is it really an independent clause?**

Yes! While the three dependent clauses in the sentence enhance the meaning of the independent clause, this dependent clause can certainly stand alone and make sense. Of course, it sounds better within the context of the entire sentence. Remember that a complex sentence must have at least one independent clause, but it may have more than one dependent clause.

Can you review complex sentences again and give more examples? It's not always easy to tell the difference between independent and dependent clauses in some sentences.

To write a complex sentence all you have to do is join an independent clause with one or more dependent clauses, using a relative pronoun or a subordinating conjunction. The independent clause presents the main idea of the sentence, and the dependent clause or clauses, although not as important, add an extra dimension to the sentence and round it out. Study this complex sentence:

The vet who boards my goldendoodle resembles a Bedlington terrier.

Once we find the dependent clause of this sentence, we can pinpoint the independent clause, the group of words that can stand alone and make sense by itself.

We already know that *who boards my goldendoodle* is the dependent clause because it starts with the relative pronoun *who* and has a subject (*who*) and a verb (*boards*). We also know that this dependent clause can't stand alone without adding a complete thought. Therefore, what's left of the sentence, *the vet resembles a Bedlington terrier*, is the independent clause.

Let's look at another complex sentence, this time one with one independent and two dependent clauses:

Because Mr. Fumbler had difficulty explaining the grammar, he slammed his book on the desk before he assigned us twenty pages of homework.

First, look for the two dependent clauses by scanning the sentence for a relative pronoun or subordinating conjunction. Since you know that *because* and *before* are subordinating conjunctions, you'll easily spot the two dependent clauses: *because Mr. Fumbler could not explain the grammar* and *before he assigned us twenty pages of homework.*

By process of elimination, you can easily find the independent clause: *he slammed his book on the desk.*

In a sentence like this, it's easier to find the dependent clause or clauses first. The clause openers (*because* and *before,* in this case) give you a hint that dependent clauses will follow.

Similarly, when the dependent clause shows up in the middle of a sentence as it did in *the vet resembles a Bedlington terrier* sentence, it's also easier to look for the dependent clause first. That will simplify your search for the independent clause.

On the other hand, when the clauses are clearly separated as they are in the following sentence, you'll probably be better off identifying the independent clause first:

As the class hooted (dependent clause), the teacher banished the class cut-up to the dean's office (independent clause).

At first glance, you'll be able to tell that the second group of words is the independent clause because it makes sense by itself and can stand alone. You have to think about it a little more in the previous two sentences.

I think I understand it now. Once you know how to identify dependent clauses, it's easy to figure out the rest of the puzzle. You talked about four types of sentences. What's the last type of sentence I need to know about?

It's called compound-complex, but now that you know the other types, you'll learn it in a flash.

It sounds like it's a combination of a compound and a complex sentence. Am I right?

Exactly. A compound-complex sentence contains two or more independent clauses and one or more dependent clauses. Here's an example:

Li won the Good Grammar Award because he knows the difference between linking and action verbs, and the teacher let him watch grammar videos all day.

Can you identify the independent clauses and the dependent clause?

That's easy. I spotted the dependent clause right away: *because he knows the difference between linking and action verbs.* **It's dependent because it begins with** *because,* **and it can't stand alone.**

The first part of the sentence, *Li won the Good Grammar Award,* **is an independent clause because it makes sense and can stand alone. The other independent clause is:** *the teacher let him watch grammar videos all day.*

Good job! You definitely understand clauses!

One final question: Is any one sentence type better than the other?

Not really. It depends on the point you're trying to make in your writing. Sometimes a stark, simple sentence drives your point home with a sharpness and clarity that you won't find in a more complicated sentence type.

However, using all simple sentences wouldn't be a good idea because your writing would get monotonous. It would also remind you of a child's first reader. On the other hand, using all compound and complex sentences may sound like a pompous professor's dissertation about how a fruit fly's brain works.

When you want to combine ideas, use a compound sentence. If you want to impart a sense of time to your sentence or make one idea stand out, you may want to use a complex sentence.

You can see that the word *when* in our complex sentence *When James asked Kia to the concert* . . . gives you a sense that James immediately got a *no* from Kia. He didn't have to wait long to find out that Kia wasn't interested in dating him.

Sometimes you may want to emphasize certain facts: for example, James asking Kia to the concert and her refusal, rather than going into the reasons why she didn't go out with him. If you use two simple sentences or a compound sentence rather than a complex sentence, you'd emphasize these facts. Adding the dependent clause could dampen the action of the two independent clauses.

Example 1 (simple sentences): James asked Kia to the concert. She said *no.*

Example 2 (compound sentence): James asked Kia to the concert, but she said *no.*

In the end, it's up to you which types of sentences you'll use. Make your sentence structure work for you. Let it shout out your message so that no one will misinterpret what you want to say. Once you feel comfortable with the different sentence types, experiment when you edit your writing. Maybe a simple sentence would work where a complex sentence wouldn't. In some cases, a complex sentence would give you just the right balance of ideas you're looking for.

Sometime when you're writing something at home for work or school and you're not under a time deadline, put a paragraph or two of your writing under the microscope. Above each sentence write whether it's *simple, compound, complex*, or *compound-complex*. Then see if you're using too many of one type of sentence. Ask yourself how changing the sentence structure would make your paragraph more interesting to your reader.

Does your paragraph seem heavy and a chore to read? Simplify, simplify! Round out your writing with some simple sentences. On the other hand, do your sentences sound like the ones kids read in their reading circle at Blue Bell Elementary? Make them more sophisticated by adding some compound, complex, and compound-complex sentences.

Try rewriting your paragraph using a variety of sentence patterns. How does it change your writing style? Which version do you like best? Read your sentences aloud. Once you try this, you'll develop an ear for what sounds good and what doesn't. Your reader will thank you.

Now it's time for two more quizzes, one on sentence types and one that gives you practice writing your own sentences. Step right up and try your luck at putting a label on the sentence types.

QUICK QUIZ #4: SENTENCE TYPES

Identify the sentence types by using these abbreviations in the space at the end of the sentence: S (simple), C (compound), CX (complex), or CC (compound-complex). Score 10 points for each correct answer.

Hot Tips

- To be called a compound sentence, each group of words must have a separate subject and a separate predicate.
- When you see a word introducing a dependent clause that you can use as a subordinating conjunction or a preposition, ask yourself if the word introduces a clause or a phrase. If it's a clause, it will contain a subject and a predicate. If it's a phrase, it will have a preposition and an object.

  1. Lionel grew a grizzly goatee, and nobody at his reunion recognized him. _____
  2. Esai played an accordion solo and danced the Hokey Pokey at his sister's wedding. _____
  3. José jumped into the ocean, and a jellyfish grabbed his big toe. _____

4. When Sandra took a day off from work, a coworker saw her go into the local spa. _____

5. After Ben threw the lobster into the boiling water, it leapt out of the pot, and it chased him around the room. _____

6. At the bachelor party, a gigantic groundhog jumped out of the cake and fell into Hector's arms. _____

7. Before she sat down in her chair, Ms. Priswell examined it for thumb-tacks, but instead she found a gift certificate from the class. _____

8. After Melissa moved to a deserted farmhouse, she bought a pit bull for protection, and she adopted a cat to kill the mice lurking in her attic. _____

9. A girl in my calculus class told the teacher that her bearded dragon lizard demolished her homework, and she grew a nose like Pinoc-chio's. _____

10. Good grammar gives your writing credibility and brings it energy. _____

QUICK QUIZ #5: WRITING DIFFERENT TYPES OF SENTENCES

Before taking another quiz on sentence types (this one asks you to write your own sentences), review the chart below to see what makes up each type of sentence.

Sentence Types: How We Build Sentences from Clauses

Simple: one independent clause

Compound: two or more independent clauses joined by a coordinating conjunction (*and, but, or*)

Complex: one independent clause and one or more dependent clauses introduced by a subordinating conjunction or a relative pronoun

Compound-Complex: two or more independent clauses plus one or more dependent clauses

After reviewing the sentence-type chart, try writing one of each type of sentence: simple, compound, complex, and compound-complex.

When your sentences are complete, check your sentences against the model sentences in the answer key.

Once you know what simple, compound, complex, and compound-complex sentences look like, make an effort to use all these different sentence types in your writing. After a period of consciously doing this, you'll become more comfortable using a variety of sentences. Armed with this knowledge and all the other new techniques you've learned, your writing style will improve dramatically.

Now that I can identify different types of sentences, how can I begin to use them in my writing?

Think about how varying some of the sentence types you write might infuse more energy into your writing.

For example, you may want to consider how adding a simple sentence at a crucial point in your writing (beginning or ending, for example) might help stress an important point you want to make.

You can give your writing more oomph by varying the kinds of sentences you write. You'll be surprised at how becoming conscious of your sentence patterns and working to change them can transform your writing from "ho hum" to "wow."

Chapter Three

Sentence Fragments and Run-On Sentences

Big-Time Blunders Corrected

Sentence fragments and run-on sentences always earn me pathetic marks in my essays: C- or worse. Help!

If you truly want to master good grammar and writing, you'll have to swear off sentence fragments and run-on sentences forever. And you'll be pleased to know that what you've learned about sentence structure will help you shun these errors like the West Nile Virus.

However, sometimes experienced writers use fragments in their writing to drive home a point or to create a mood. But it's best not to use fragments until you're sure that you have a good understanding of sentence structure, which you're gaining right now.

Here's a surefire way to help you quickly decide if you've written a fragment. Every sentence needs at least one complete thought (independent clause). If it doesn't have a complete thought, you've probably concocted a grammatical monster, a sentence fragment.

Fragments come in all shapes and sizes. Many fragments are dependent clauses in disguise, so check to see if your sentence makes sense. Try reading it aloud to a friend. If the person you're reading it to frowns, squints, or says, "Run that by me again," you've probably composed a fragment rather than a complete sentence.

Here's an example of a dependent clause fragment:

Because Bertram always threw gutter balls.

You're probably wondering, "Where's the rest of the sentence? It sounds like something's missing." If you add a strong independent clause to this weak dependent clause, you'll create a complete thought. Would you like to try?

Sure. Here's what I'd write: *Because Bertram always threw gutter balls, his buddies named him bowling bungler of the year.*

Now here's the true test of your understanding. What makes what you wrote a sentence? What makes the first part of the sentence a fragment if it stands alone?

It's simple. The first clause, *Because Bertram always threw gutter balls,* **is a dependent clause. It can't stand alone, and it doesn't make sense by itself. But when I add the independent clause,** *his buddies named him bowling bungler of the year,* **it's a complete sentence, not a fragment.**

Perfect! Here's another fragment, this time a prepositional phrase fragment: *In the lake across the street.* How would you turn it into a sentence?

How about this? *In the lake across the street, a fifteen-foot alligator bared its eighty teeth at me.* **And before you ask—all I did was add an independent clause to turn it into a sentence.**

I believe you're quickly becoming a grammar expert. But before you get carried away, remember that fragments aren't always dependent clauses or prepositional phrases. Sometimes they're groups of words that are missing a verb (*Egg on her face,* for example).

Other times, fragments begin with action words ending in *ing,* and they're called *participial phrases*:

Hooting and hollering when the home team scored a basket.

If you added more words, this phrase would morph into a sentence:

Hooting and hollering when the home team scored a basket, the fans showed their loyalty to their team.

Fragments show up in the strangest places and sometimes look remarkably like sentences. The one thing they all have in common is that they need to hook up with an independent clause or they won't make sense.

Do you have any advice for avoiding run-on sentences? When I'm writing, I sometimes start rambling. I get carried away and don't know when to stop.

Run-on sentences, like sentence fragments, are often caused because writers don't take the time to proofread. If you go over what you write and check to see that every sentence has at least one complete thought, you'll never strike out with a fragment. However, if you look at your writing and see that you have *more* than one complete thought not joined by the proper punctuation or a conjunction, you're looking at a run-on sentence.

How can punctuation help me zap run-on sentences?

To separate independent clauses you need something stronger than a comma. Try a semicolon, a conjunction, or a period. Here's an example of a run-on sentence separated with a comma:

Andre stayed in the hot tub too long, his skin withered like a weather-beaten warthog's.

You can see that this sentence has two separate thoughts, two independent clauses. How would you doctor it up with punctuation to make it a legitimate sentence?

I'd put a period after *long* and make it two sentences, or I could add *and* after *long* and make it a compound sentence.

Good solutions! Another thing you could do is add a semicolon after *long*. It's a little stronger than a comma and a bit weaker than a period, but it will work equally well. The semicolon takes the place of the conjunction *and*.

Example: Andre stayed in the hot tub too long; his skin withered like a weather-beaten warthog's.

What else do I need to know about run-ons?

Another type of run-on sentence uses no punctuation at all. The writer rambles on and forgets that every good sentence must come to an end. Take a look at this monstrosity:

Lana's pet parakeet slept in a doll bed every morning he flew to her room and woke her up by chirping "Reveille."

Can you give that sentence first aid?

I tried reading the sentence aloud to see how it would sound. I decided to put a period or a semicolon after *bed*. I don't think it would sound right to use *and* or *but* in this sentence because the sentence would seem too long and drawn out.

I agree with both of your solutions. That proves that it's a good idea to read aloud what you write and listen to the sentence rhythm. Experiment with your sentences until you find what works for you. Trust your judgment.

I'd say you're ready for a quiz on sentence fragments and run-on sentences.

QUICK QUIZ #6: SENTENCE FRAGMENTS AND RUN-ON SENTENCES

After each group of words, write sentence fragment (SF), run-on (RO), or complete sentence (CS). When you see italicized words, identify the specific error these words represent.

1. Jane made her husband sign a contract. *That he would clean the house from top to bottom every week.* _____
2. Marc presented Hannah with the "Employee of the Month" award, she refused to wear the cardboard crown and carry the magic wand. _____
3. Luisa was enjoying her hamburger until her boyfriend told her the "burger" was actually black beans and horseradish. _____
4. Dora, the Dalmatian, was ravenously hungry she ate the six barbecued pork chops we'd left on the counter for dinner. _____
5. The student blowing bubbles as big as his face. _____
6. Shawn sat in the car's front seat and let out a few noisy burps, he didn't realize that his sophisticated new girlfriend sitting in the backseat heard the entire performance. _____
7. Because Lena wouldn't tell her fiancé if she went out with another man. He hired a private detective. _____
8. After Sal fell asleep during the lesson on demonstrative pronouns, his teacher threw a bucket of water on him to wake him. _____
9. Danielle painted a portrait of her boss he didn't like the fact that his nose resembled a woodpecker's. _____
10. Tomás cooked deer meat for his family, but he told them they were eating roasted chicken. _____

Chapter Four

Adjectives and Adverbs

How to Use Them Wisely

I'd like to learn more about describing words or modifiers, such as adjectives and adverbs. I always thought my writing would look better (more descriptive) if I sprinkled my essays with lots of adjectives and adverbs. However, my teacher thought that I overused them and said I needed to find other ways of making my writing more interesting.

Before we discuss adjectives and adverbs, let's address your teacher's concerns about overusing them in writing. Most writing teachers agree that it's better to depend on nouns and verbs to make your writing more descriptive and lively.

Adjectives and adverbs have their place, but whenever you can, let specific nouns and strong active verbs carry your sentence. Here are some examples: *convertible* or *CRV* instead of *car* (specific versus general nouns) and *meander* instead of *walk slowly* (strong versus weak verb).

This is not to say that you should always steer clear of using adjectives and adverbs in your prose. Occasionally, an adjective or adverb can enhance a sentence. For the most part, however, let your nouns and verbs carry the weight of your sentences.

Use your best instincts to tell you when to use adjectives and adverbs. Read your sentence aloud. Would it sound better if you used a strong noun or verb, or would the adjective or adverb work better? In most cases, experienced writers would opt for the strong noun or verb.

It's also important to know that modifiers can show up in the form of phrases. Phrases function the same way that one-word describing words do in sentences. You've already learned about prepositional phrases. You've also learned the endings for the past and present participle forms of verbs: *ed, d, en,* and *n* for the past, and *ing* for the present participle.

When you see groups of words with these endings describing a word in a sentence, they're called participial phrases. Knowing about different types of phrases will come in handy so that you aren't tempted to commit the unspeakable error of using a dangling participle or misplaced modifier.

It's a good time to mention that there's another type of phrase called a gerund phrase. A gerund is a verbal word (for example, *singing* and *dancing*) that acts as a noun. It can show up as a subject, object, predicate nominative (the word that follows a linking verb), or the object of a preposition.

Some grammarians don't make a big deal over the difference between gerund phrases and participial phrases. They look similar, don't you think?

The simple fact is that gerund phrases are always used as nouns (subjects, objects, predicate nominatives, and objects of the preposition) in a sentence, while participial phrases are used as adjectives to describe nouns.

To clarify, here's an example of a participial phrase:

Gobbling up the roast beef, my King Charles spaniel gave me a guilty look as I entered the kitchen.

Gobbling up the roast beef is a participial phrase describing my King Charles spaniel, the subject of the sentence. It's used as an adjective so it's a participial phrase, not a gerund phrase, which you'll only see acting as a noun in a sentence.

Compare the participial phrase with the use of a gerund in this sentence:

My King Charles spaniel enjoyed gobbling up the roast beef.

In this example, *gobbling up the roast beef* is used as a noun. It's the object of *enjoyed*, so it's a gerund phrase.

Before you learn how any of these different types of modifiers can add unwanted humor to your sentences, you'll want to know how to identify adjectives and adverbs in their basic form.

DESCRIPTIVE AND LIMITING ADJECTIVES

To start off, an adjective describes nouns in a sentence. There are two kinds of adjectives: descriptive and limiting. Descriptive adjectives tell us something about a noun (the *active* child, a *savory* stew, and the *endless* highway).

It's easy to remember limiting adjectives because there are only three: *a*, *an*, and *the*. Sometimes you'll want to use proper adjectives to describe nouns; in this case, you'll use a capital letter.

Example: The *Italian* marble enhanced our dated kitchen fixtures.

You can also find adjectives after a linking verb:

Example: Sasha was so *spunky* that no one could control her.

Incidentally, if you're writing a short story or a personal essay, most writing experts would advise you to show *how* the child demonstrates her spunkiness rather than to simply say that she was spunky.

You can show rather than tell by giving an example of how the child acted and then letting the reader figure out that she was indeed a spunky child. Here's a sample sentence that shows rather than tells:

Sasha bounded up to the podium and implored the school board to keep the music program in her school.

In this sentence, you could also say *strongly urged* instead of *implored*, but why use two words when one will give the same message?

If you don't like the sound of the word *implored* or think your readers may not know what it means, use a synonym like *petitioned*. Many times you'll find that the words you use are personal judgment calls.

Whenever you write, ask yourself what choice of words would make your readers understand what you're saying with the least effort on their part. The more you read and write, the more you'll start to get a feel for what works and what doesn't to help your readers understand the message you're trying to convey.

My teacher said it would help to go through my writing and eliminate all words ending in *ly* because they're adverbs. Isn't that a little extreme?

You may have noticed that not all adverbs end in *ly* (*here*, *there*, and *well*, for example, as in *I am well*). When you come across a word that tells something about the action word (*how*, *how much, in what way*, *when*, and *where*), it's an adverb.

Adverbs can also modify adjectives:
That outfit is *very* stylish.

Adverbs can modify other adverbs:
> **You understand grammar *extremely* well.**

Adverbs can also modify nouns.
> **They held their political rallies in the lounge *upstairs*.**

To answer your question about ridding your writing of all adverbs, I'd say try to use strong verbs whenever you can and use adverbs sparingly. Adverbs often weigh sentences down and make it easy for you to avoid searching for a strong verb that will keep your reader engaged in your writing. In other words, avoid adverbs and look for the most powerful verbs to make your writing powers soar.

If I do use an adverb, where's the best place to put it in a sentence?
Position an adverb as close as you can to the word it's modifying. Sometimes you can put an adverb in different places in a sentence to emphasize different meanings. Here's an example using the adverb *also*:

> **I will *also* make a video of our karaoke party.**

This implies that you'll do something in addition to making the video.
Put *also* in another place, and you'll get a different meaning. Think about this sentence:

> **I *also* will make a video of our karaoke party.**

This means that you and other people will make a video of the party. You can see that the sentence meaning depends on the placement of the adverb.
You can change your sentence's meaning by placing adverbs in different positions in a sentence. Try experimenting with placement of ones that often change sentence meaning, such as *only*, *also*, *not*, *barely*, *just*, and *however*.
It also helps to remember not to separate the infinitive (*to* plus the verb) with the word *only* as in: **Marcus wants to *only* go to the play with Elaina.** *Only* breaks up the infinitive *to go* in this sentence, and you'll want to avoid that because it sounds awkward. It's better to say **Marcus only wants to go to the play with Elaina.**
Most strict grammarians believe that splitting an infinitive (*to* plus the verb) marks you as someone who doesn't have a clue about grammar. Avoid splitting infinitives if you're writing an application letter for a job that will require you to have first-rate grammar skills or if you're writing an essay for a professor with impeccable standards.

Chapter Five

Dangling and Misplaced Modifiers

How to Identify and Avoid Them

DANGLING MODIFIERS

There are a couple of other errors that have always baffled me. My teacher once said, "Excuse me, your participle's dangling." I had no idea what she meant, and I felt embarrassed when she said that in front of the entire class. Everyone, including the teacher, got a good laugh at my expense.

Just as you need to put a single adjective or adverb close to the word it modifies, it's important to place participial and prepositional phrases or modifying clauses correctly in the sentence. If you don't, you could find yourself using a dangling or misplaced modifier.

Despite her insensitivity, your English teacher was right about dangling modifiers. These sentence foul-ups can make your sentences read like bad one-liners at Comedy Central.

Humor wouldn't be the best tone to use if you were writing a letter of complaint to "Crabby's Fish Fry" about the stomach distress you suffered after gobbling up their fried clam strips. You'd definitely want your modifiers to be in the right place.

Here's how one customer phrased her misadventure with the restaurant:

After eating your greasy clam strips, my stomach did cartwheels and flip-flops.

The first part of the sentence, *after eating your greasy clam strips*, a phrase, doesn't describe anything. Reading the sentence makes you believe that your stomach ate the clam strips. Maybe the clams ended up there, but your stomach didn't actually eat them.

This klutzy group of words can't do anything but dangle. If they had good sense, these words would find a word to attach themselves to in the sentence; in other words, they would think of a word to modify.

Can you think of a way to correct this sentence?

Let's try this: *After eating your greasy clam strips, I could feel my stomach doing cartwheels and flip-flops.*

I'd say that's a good solution because now you're letting the phrase modify the noun *I*. Let's look at another example of a dangling modifier:

Scaling fish and pounding meat, the waitstaff listened to the chef's complaints about working in a sweatshop.

Notice how the introductory phrase doesn't modify anything but seems to refer to the waitstaff. The words before the comma dangle, wanting desperately to attach themselves to other words that will help them make better sense.

Here's one way you can correct the sentence:

While scaling fish and pounding meat, the chef complained to the waitstaff about working in a sweatshop.

This revamped sentence now attaches itself to the noun and subject of the independent clause, *chef*, and functions as an adjective modifying *chef*.

Here's another dangling modifier, this time using the present participle of the verb *flash*:

Flashing on his computer screen, Diego read a "Dear John" e-mail from his girlfriend.

Was Diego's sad face flashing on the computer screen? If it wasn't, you'll want to change the sentence to read something like this:

Diego read his girlfriend's "Dear John" e-mail as it flashed on his computer screen.

Are there other types of dangling modifiers that cause problems with sentence meaning?

Although participles often introduce dangling modifiers, other types of dangling modifiers sometimes appear in sentences.

Here's an example of a dangling modifier introduced by an infinitive phrase (*to* plus the verb):

To master grammar, common sense and a sense of humor are needed.

Based on what you now know about dangling modifiers, how would you correct this sentence?

I'd change it to: *To master grammar, a student needs common sense and a sense of humor.* **I don't want to act like a know-it-all, but I also noticed that the original sentence is in passive voice.**

You're right. It is passive voice! If it's helping you see an example of a dangling modifier, we won't worry about it this time. By the way, I like the way you changed the sentence to active voice.

Here's another example of a dangling modifier.

After dancing all night, our muscles ached.

See what you can do to eliminate the dangling modifier.

This one's easy! The way the sentence stands, it makes it seem that the muscles danced. I'd change it to: *After dancing all night, we had achy muscles.*

Right again! I believe that you can correct any dangling modifier that someone throws your way. Here's another one for you.

Gabbing constantly to his friends during the meeting, the boss rated Gus unsatisfactory.

I don't think the boss would gab constantly during the meeting, so I'd say: *Gabbing constantly to his friends during the meeting, Gus was rated unsatisfactory.*

Correct! You can see how illogical the sentence sounds with the dangling modifier.

MISPLACED MODIFIERS

Am I right in saying that misplaced modifiers would be easier to fix than dangling modifiers? From what I can see, dangling modifiers are all over the place, while misplaced modifiers seem to be in the wrong place.

In most cases, it is easier to fix misplaced modifiers because all you have to do is change some words around. You don't have to add words or make changes to the sentence as you sometimes have to with dangling modifiers. You'll find that you can usually correct a misplaced modifier by positioning the modifiers as close as possible to the words they describe.

Often writers misplace one-word modifiers such as *only*, *just*, *namely*, or *barely*.

The following sentence can have two meanings, depending on where you place the modifier:

Maria was *just* chosen to give the graduation speech. (This means that she was recently chosen.)

Maria was chosen to give *just* the graduation speech. (This means that the only thing Maria will do is give the graduation speech.)

Here are examples of a modifier having two meanings, using *only*:

Leah's sister *only* offered her $20 if she would disappear when Leah's boyfriend visited. (She only *offered* her sister the money. Who knew if she would pay?)
Leah's sister offered her *only* $20 if she would disappear when Leah's boyfriend visited. (Leah's sister probably wanted more money to make her disappear!)

Here's the bottom line: Put the modifier as close as possible to the word it modifies to help readers know exactly what you mean.

Often, you'll see a misplaced modifier that has more than one word. Try correcting this misplaced clause modifier:

I liked the picture of you and your fiancé in the trolley that you sent me.

I wouldn't want to give the impression that you sent me a trolley. I'd say: *I liked the picture that you sent me of you and your fiancé in the trolley.*

That's a good answer! Here's an example of a phrase modifier and an easy way to correct it:

Incorrect: Portia's missing luggage was sent by an airline worker in a large cardboard box.

Correct: An airline worker sent Portia's missing luggage in a large cardboard box.

The first sentence makes it look like the airline worker was hiding inside the cardboard box! I also see the passive voice in the incorrect sentence.

I'm glad that you again recognized the passive voice, which you need to use sparingly in writing.

Let's look at one more misplaced modifier (a clause modifier, this time) and see how to correct it:

Incorrect: Max wore flip-flops on his aching feet that he had bought at the dollar store.

Correct: On his aching feet Max wore flip-flops that he had bought at the dollar store.

The first sentence makes it look like Max bought his feet at the dollar store!

And you wouldn't want your reader to think that! You can see how dangling and misplaced modifiers can sometimes interfere with sentence sense and how fixing them can pose a challenge. Now it's time for Quick Quiz #7.

QUICK QUIZ #7: DANGLING AND MISPLACED MODIFIERS

Name the error. Write DM for dangling modifier and MM for misplaced modifier. Correct the sentence by rewriting it. See suggested answers in the answer key. There may be more than one way to correct the sentences. Each question carries 10 points, 5 for the name of the error and 5 for the correction.

Hot Tip

- Remember that a dangling modifier dangles and doesn't describe anything, while a misplaced modifier shows up in the wrong place in a sentence.

1. I borrowed a book from my teacher that contained pages of mind-deadening grammar exercises.

    Error: _____

    Sentence Rewrite:

    _____

2. After studying all night, our eyes drooped the next morning.

    Error: _____

    Sentence Rewrite:

    _____

3. Looking out the window, a purple-haired clown on stilts caught my eye.

    Error: _____

    Sentence Rewrite:

    _____

4. Marisol was stung by a bee riding a skateboard.

    Error: _____

    Sentence Rewrite:

    _____

5. Explain the meaning of *only* in each sentence:

    The dog *only* howled while I was sleeping.

    _____

    The dog howled *only* while I was sleeping.

    _____

    Sentence Rewrite:

    _____

6. Attached to his backpack, John saw a parking ticket.

Error: _____

Sentence Rewrite:

_____

7. Juliet's roses were delivered by the florist in a porcelain vase.

Error: _____

Sentence Rewrite:

_____

8. While walking on the beach, a jellyfish stung my big toe.

Error: _____

Sentence Rewrite:

_____

9. At the age of six my mother gave me a silver scooter.

Error: _____

Sentence Rewrite:

_____

10. There was a rose bush next to the septic tank that smelled very fragrant.

Error: _____

Sentence Rewrite:

_____

Chapter Six

Commas, Part I

How They Help Sentences Make Sense

Knowing about clauses, different sentence types, and modifiers is helping me write better, but my punctuation's terrible. Help!

Let's start with the comma because that little mark seems to give students the most trouble. It's surprising because when I tell students to read their writing aloud, they'll sometimes know instinctively when to use commas.

Although some students use this method successfully, even the best writers aren't always sure about when to insert a comma. That's why it helps to know the rules. Remember—don't memorize. Read the rules with the goal of understanding them, and look over the examples. Soon they'll make sense to you, and if you couple your understanding of the rules with your common sense, you'll begin to get a feeling for proper punctuation.

You mentioned earlier that knowing about clauses can help me with punctuation.

Let's talk first about using commas in compound sentences, that is, in sentences where you see independent clauses linked with conjunctions (*and, but, or, for, nor, yet,* and *so*). Place the comma before the conjunction. If the independent clauses are very short, you don't have to use a comma.

Here's an example of two independent clauses joined by a conjunction using a comma:

Antonio's groomsmen planned his bachelor party, and they all competed to find the silliest gag gifts.

Here's another sentence. Can you figure out why you don't need a comma?

43

I aimed the bowling ball at the pins and saw the ball head toward the gutter.

I remember from Chapter Two that you can have compound subjects and predicates. That doesn't mean it's a compound sentence. In a compound sentence you need two separate subjects and two separate predicates. This sentence has a compound predicate (*aimed/saw*), so I think it's a simple sentence. There's no subject before *saw*. You can't have a compound sentence unless there are separate subjects and predicates for *each* independent clause.

I'm glad you remembered that! Here's an example of two independent clauses joined by a conjunction in a compound-complex sentence.

After Chung ate the chocolate-covered grasshoppers, her stomach began to flutter, and she had a strong urge to hop.

In this compound-complex sentence you'll need a comma before *and* because it joins two independent clauses: *her stomach began to flutter* and *she had a strong urge to hop.* Also, if you read the sentence, you'll naturally pause after the dependent clause when you read the sentence. A pause prompts you to put in a comma.

Do you always have to put a comma after a dependent clause?

Knowing about clauses will definitely help you punctuate complex sentences. When you see a dependent clause in the beginning of a sentence, put a comma after it. When the dependent clause shows up at the end of a sentence, you don't need a comma before it.

Note the position of the dependent clauses in the following two sentences and see how the first one, positioned at the beginning of the sentence, needs a comma, but the second one, which comes at the end, doesn't.

Example 1: If I don't learn sentence structure now, I'll spend the rest of my life deciding how to punctuate sentences.

Use a comma if the dependent clause shows up in the beginning of the sentence.

Example 2: I'll spend the rest of my life deciding how to punctuate sentences if I don't learn about sentence structure now.

Don't use a comma if the dependent clause shows up at the end of the sentence.

Omit the comma in sentences with short clauses like the ones in the sentence below.

I overate and I paid for it later.

Sure, it's still compound, but you can say it in a flash, and you don't need to pause when you read it, so why bother embellishing it with a comma?

THE DIFFERENCE BETWEEN CLAUSES AND PHRASES

Sometimes I still have trouble figuring out the difference between clauses and phrases in a sentence. I've also heard that I have to use a comma with some prepositional phrases but not with others. Please explain.

In Chapter Two we talked about the fact that you can use some (but not all) of the same words as prepositional phrases or subordinating conjunctions. To review, a phrase is nothing more than a group of words that has a subject and a predicate that you can use as a part of speech, such as an adjective or adverb.

First, let's talk about prepositional phrases in a little more detail. Before we discuss prepositional phrases, you'll want to look over a list of prepositions, and here they are:

about, above, across, after, against, along, amid, among, around, at, before, behind, below, beneath, beside, besides, between, beyond, but (meaning *except*), by, down, during, except, for, from, in, inside, into, like, near, of, off, on, out, outside, over, past, since, through, throughout, to, toward, under, underneath, until, unto, up, upon, with, within, and without.

Remember—familiarize, don't memorize.

The key to knowing whether you're looking at a phrase or a clause is in knowing what ingredients each one has. Remember that if the introductory word is followed by a subject and a predicate, it's a *dependent clause,* but if the introductory word has an object rather than a subject and verb, it's a prepositional phrase.

Take a look at these examples:

Dependent Clause: Before I went to the holiday party, I filled up on fruit and yogurt so I wouldn't pig out on chips and dips, deep-fried turkey, and tiramisu. (*Before* is a subordinating conjunction.)

Prepositional Phrase: Before the holiday party I filled up on fruit and yogurt so I wouldn't pig out on chips and dips, deep-fried turkey, and tiramisu. (*Before* is a preposition.)

In the first example, the first part of the sentence is a dependent clause. Insert a comma after the introductory dependent clause. In the second example, there's no comma after *party* because *before the holiday party* is a prepositional phrase.

Remember to use a comma when you see **two or more introductory prepositional phrases**. When there's only one prepositional phrase, as in the previous sentence example, you don't need to use a comma unless you need it to clarify the sentence meaning.

Example 1: On the second floor near the stairwells, friends chatted with one another between classes. (two prepositional phrases, *on the second floor* and *near the stairwells*: Use a comma.)

Example 2: Behind the door a frightening monster lurked and suddenly lunged at us. (one prepositional phrase, *behind the door*: Don't use a comma.)

Are there any other types of phrases I should know how to punctuate with a comma?

APPOSITIVES WITH AND WITHOUT COMMAS

Another type of phrase that figures in comma usage is the appositive phrase. It consists of an appositive and its modifiers. An appositive is a word or group of words that explains or renames a noun or pronoun. The words following the appositive mean the same thing as the appositive.

Example: Ms. Zany, my favorite English teacher, wore polka-dotted bell-bottoms and sported an "English nut" tattoo on her arm.
In this sentence the appositive phrase *my favorite English teacher* tells us who Ms. Zany is, so we set off these words with commas.

Sometimes an appositive shows up as only one word that's closely related to the word it modifies. In cases like this, don't use a comma.

Example: The word *grammar* used to send chills down my spine.

In this sentence *grammar* is the appositive that refers back to *word*. It's important to the sentence meaning, so we don't set it off with a comma. As in many cases, reading the sentence aloud will help you know whether to use a comma.

Try reading the sentence with and without a pause before and after *grammar*. You'll see that you don't need to pause and rightly decide not to use a comma.

Here are more examples of one-word appositives that don't need a comma. We call them *restrictive appositives* because they restrict the meaning of the sentence, which means they don't need a comma.

> my aunt Caprice
> the beat generation poet Ferlinghetti
> the word *kerfuffle*

Let's look at another example of a restrictive appositive with more than one word:

The opening scene of the novel *The Catcher in the Rye* takes place in a mental hospital.

In this sentence the title of the book restricts the meaning of the sentence, so we don't use a comma. We need the book title to know which novel we're discussing.

Contrast this with an appositive that doesn't restrict the meaning of a sentence:

***The Catcher in the Rye*, a novel read in many schools, chronicles the adventures of Holden Caulfield, a young man who had difficulty coping with the stresses in his life.**

In this sentence we use commas because the appositive doesn't restrict the sentence meaning. It's common knowledge that many students read this novel in school. In the second part of the sentence, we put a comma after the words Holden Caulfield because the part that follows is additional information. The main point is that the novel chronicles the adventures of Holden Caulfield who had trouble dealing with the stresses in his life.

Here's an example of a sentence in which you can consider the appositive restrictive if you write it one way and nonrestrictive if you write it another way.

Restrictive Appositive: The dance troupe Rock 'Til You Drop appeared at the concert hall.

Rock 'Til You Drop is a restrictive appositive because it's important to the meaning of the sentence. We want to know which dance troupe appeared at the hall. That's why we don't use a comma. If we used a comma, we'd be saying that any old dance troupe appeared, and we want to specify the one that did.

Nonrestrictive Appositive: Rock 'Til You Drop, the dance troupe, appeared at the concert hall.

In this sentence we use a comma because we're counting on the fact that everyone knows about Rock 'Til You Drop, the dance troupe (what—you've never heard of them?). Therefore, in this sentence we can consider the appositive nonrestrictive and set it off with commas.

To sum it up, knowing whether you need commas to set off an appositive is sometimes a judgment call. Just ask yourself if the sentence could make sense without the appositive or if it's additional information. If it is, then it's nonrestrictive and you'll need commas.

Later, we're going to look at some examples of restrictive and nonrestrictive clauses and phrases. It's basically the same principle.

COMMAS IN A SERIES

What other comma rules do I need to know besides the ones related to clauses and phrases?

Another comma rule relates to items in a series, which is simply a list of three or more items listed in a sentence. Here's an example of commas in a series:

Shane bought these items at the grocery store: chicken, sweet potatoes, ice pops, and gummy bunnies.

Sometimes each item in a series can be more than one or two words. As with a shorter series, you'll still put commas after each item. Here's an example:

Willie told his girlfriend that he couldn't get engaged because he didn't have money for a ring, his mother would cry if he left, and he was afraid of her terrible temper.

You don't have to include a comma before the *and* that introduces the last item in the series. If you want to put in this last comma before the final *and*, do it all the time, or skip it altogether, but be consistent.

Also, some colleges and businesses ask you to conform to a certain style. If so, follow the advice of the recommended style manual when deciding whether to use that final comma.

When you read the sentence examples above, you'll naturally pause after each word in the series, and that means it's a good idea to insert commas after all the items—unless you've decided to follow the style that says leave out the final comma before the conjunction.

If you don't pay attention to the commas in the sample sentences above and run all the words together, you'll sound as if you're trying to pronounce one of those tongue twisters, such as *Peter Piper picked a peck of pickled peppers*, that leaves you babbling.

Finally, you don't need to use commas when all the words in a series are joined with *or*, *nor*, or *and*.

I remember seeing sentences where there weren't commas before all the adjectives that describe a noun. Please explain.

When the last adjective before the noun is so closely related to the noun that you can think of it as a single idea, you don't need a comma between the two adjectives.

Example: The fragrant spring flowers enhanced the elegant banquet table.

In the first part of this sentence, we think of *spring flowers* as one idea; therefore, don't put a comma between *fragrant* and *spring.*

Similarly, in the second part of this sentence, *banquet table* is thought of as a single idea rather than two separate words. Therefore, you don't need a comma after *elegant* because *banquet table* is considered one entity.

Also, it helps to think about how you'd read this sentence aloud. In the first instance, it would sound awkward if you paused after *fragrant*. In the second, it wouldn't sound right if you paused after *elegant.*

Is there any way you can help me definitely know when to use a comma with adjectives?

To further help when you have a question about using a comma with adjectives before nouns, here's a test you can use: try inserting the word *and* between the adjectives. If *and* fits between the two adjectives, use a comma. In our example it wouldn't sound right to say *fragrant* and *spring* or *elegant* and *banquet*, so you can omit the comma here.

COMMAS IN DIRECT ADDRESS

What are some other uses of the comma?

Another common use for the comma is **direct address**. Whenever you call a person or a group by name, set off the name or title with a comma.

Example: "Class, if I see any of you in remedial college English next year, I'll know I've failed," Mr. Persnickety proclaimed as he droned on for the rest of the period about commas and colons.

Notice how this example shows the commonsense rule that you can use in so many cases of punctuation. Read the sentence aloud, and you'll know instinctively that you pause after *class*.

COMMAS WITH INTRODUCTORY WORDS

You'll also need a comma after introductory words like *yes, no, well*, and *oh*. Here are two sentences using a comma after an introductory word:

Example 1: "*No*, I won't accept late homework because your Internet tutor decided to take a break from answering questions from grammatically challenged students last night," said Ms. Irascible.

Example 2: "*Yes*, of course I love you madly," Manny told his girlfriend as he absentmindedly devoured the box of chocolates he'd given her for her birthday.

Notice how these examples show the commonsense rule that you can use in so many cases of punctuation. Read the sentences aloud, and you'll know instinctively that you pause after *no* and *yes*.

Remember: If you pause when you say it, pause when you write it.

Using your ear for good grammar helped you figure out where to place commas in the sentences above. If you're ever in doubt about whether to use a comma, try reading the sentence aloud.

Notice that when you pause or when your inflection changes (your voice goes up or down), you'll probably use a comma. Be aware of how you say a sentence aloud, and often you'll know how to punctuate it with other punctuation marks as well. Naturally, there are exceptions, but trust your instincts along with your good grammar sense when deciding how to punctuate, and they'll carry you a long way.

COMMAS WITH TRANSITION WORDS

What about those words like *however* that I've heard help you organize paragraphs? My teacher told me that using them would help make my writing easier to follow.

Your teacher was talking about *transition words*, sometimes called *parenthetical expressions.* These words tighten up your writing because they help you tie ideas together in paragraphs and allow for a smooth progression from one paragraph to another. Using them in exams, research papers, and professional reports will mark you as an expert at organizing your writing to make it reader-friendly.

Transitions or parenthetical expressions add incidental information or help relate one idea to another. When they relate ideas, you usually place them at the beginning of the sentence. Transitions are like guideposts, alerting readers to what they're going to see next in an essay or report.

Here are some of the most common transition words: *after, consequently, for example, for instance, however, in my opinion, nevertheless, of course, on the other hand, therefore, finally,* and *in conclusion.* These expressions can show up in different places in sentences. Note the different positions in these two sentences:

Example 1: *However,* if you'd rather take another semester of English, Professor Grammarian will be glad to register you for his scintillating syntax class.

The word *however* helps prepare your reader for what's to follow. It lets you know that some kind of opposing thought from what went before will follow. When you read this sentence, notice how your voice pauses naturally after *however.* That means you'll need a comma.

Example 2: If you try the snapper soup, you will, I believe, enjoy it despite the fact that it comes from a turtle.

In this sentence you need to set off the parenthetical expression, *I believe*, with commas. Notice how your voice lowers when you say these words. In some cases you'll pause, and in others, like the previous sentence, you'll lower the tone of your voice. These subtle changes in how you read a sentence are both signs that prompt you to use a comma. Be aware of how you say a sentence aloud, and often you'll know how to punctuate it.

COMMAS IN DATES AND ADDRESSES

Tell me about commas between dates and addresses.

When you see dates and addresses, put a comma after every element except for the state and the zip code. In dates, you don't need a comma if only the month and year are given, as in *December 2054.*

Punctuate dates this way: Friday, June 14, is graduation day.

Punctuate addresses this way: Professor D. Participle, 800 Plugaway Plaza, Princeton, NJ 17178

Now you're ready for a quiz on commas, which covers all the rules you've learned so far.

QUICK QUIZ #8: COMMAS

On a sheet of paper, write the name of the comma rule and the word before the comma. Use the abbreviations listed below if the sentence requires a comma. Then write the word that goes before the comma. Write NC (no comma) if the sentence doesn't need commas. Some sentences involve two comma uses. (Sentences with more than one comma use are identified.)

The comma quiz contains 100 points, so score 5 points for each correct answer or simply write the number wrong at the top of the page. Give yourself credit for each comma you use and for the reason you use it.

Here's a list of comma rules we've covered and their abbreviations: CC (before coordinating conjunctions used to separate independent clauses); DC (after dependent clauses in the beginning of sentences); Prep P (after two or more introductory prepositional phrases); I (introductory word); AP (appositives); CS (commas in a series); DA (direct address); PE (parenthetical expression); D and A (dates and addresses), and DA (direct address).

Here's an example of how you'll write your answers:

Whenever it rains I spend the morning eating a half-dozen doughnuts and I spend the afternoon working out at the gym. (two errors)

Answer:

1. DC: rains,
2. CC: donuts,

You can see that the first example is an introductory dependent clause; that means you put a comma after *rains*. The second part of the answer shows a compound sentence. That means you use a comma after *doughnuts* because you're separating two independent clauses joined by a conjunction.

Now let the quiz begin!

1. "Yes you were the student who tapped out the answers to the multiple-choice test on the desk and now I've caught you," said Dr. Severe. (2 rules)
2. When Cruz concocted a story about having a prehistoric animal for a pet his gullible friend believed him.
3. My boss Agnes named me employee of the year because I stocked her desk drawer with macadamia nut cookies.
4. Beneath a dark cave in the craggy mountains we searched for the prehistoric creature.
5. Miranda Malarkey a teller of tall tales told her boss that her cat died her car battery failed and her little toe broke so that she wouldn't have to work a double shift. (2 rules)
6. "In my opinion the memo you wrote could offend many people," the angry CEO told her assistant.
7. If you don't want to e-mail me send a letter to Apartment 767 Honey-suckle Road Philadelphia PA 19178. (2 rules)
8. The ferocious Yorkshire terrier leaped out from behind the couch and nibbled my toes.
9. "Jayden why did I see you at the mall when you were supposed to be working?" the boss asked.
10. "I wondered why you were there too but I didn't dare ask," Jayden answered.
11. Rafael devoured two cheeseburgers fries and a chocolate milkshake but he ran around the track twenty times to make up for it. (2 rules)
12. At the company dinner Portia got bored and started texting on her smartphone when the conversation turned to widgets.

13. We held the company holiday party at 516 Fifth Avenue Naples Florida.
14. Mabel my grandmother's best friend ran a marathon at eighty and she came out in first place. (2 rules)
15. The tiny toy poodle was so small that I carried her in my purse.

Chapter Seven

Commas, Part II

How to Punctuate Restrictive and Nonrestrictive Clauses and Phrases

One of my teachers spent a week talking about restrictive and nonrestrictive clauses and phrases. I found it complicated and tuned her out. Now I want to know more about how this relates to commas.

When we talked about restrictive and nonrestrictive appositives, I said that if an appositive restricted the sentence's meaning, you wouldn't use a comma. However, if the appositive just presented extra information or wasn't necessary to make the sentence clear, it was considered a nonrestrictive appositive and you *would* use a comma.

It's the same with clauses and phrases in a sentence. Use a comma if you believe the clause or phrase adds information, but don't use one if you believe the information is vital to the sentence meaning.

Look at a couple of examples and ask yourself whether the dependent clauses in the sentences restrict (change) the meaning of the sentences. If the sentences wouldn't have the same meaning without the dependent clauses, you can call these clauses restrictive, and you won't need a comma.

Example of a restrictive clause (no comma):

Students who participate in food fights will be banned from the cafeteria.

In this sentence the clause *who participate in food fights* restricts or changes the sentence's meaning. You're not implying that *all* students will be banned from the cafeteria. You're saying that only students who participate in food fights will be banned from eating with the rest of the kids who know how to act civilized.

In sentences like this where the dependent clause adds important information that **restricts** sentence meaning, you don't need a comma because the information contained in the clause is important to the sentence meaning. If something's important, you don't set it off with commas.

Here's another example of a restrictive clause (no comma):

The grammar that I learn in this book will help me write better.

The clause *that I learn in this book* is restrictive; therefore, the sentence requires no commas. Note that dependent clauses introduced by *that* are always restrictive.

Example of a nonrestrictive clause (comma):

There are certain unwritten laws in the workplace, which everyone instinctively knows, that can make you either a valued employee or one headed for a pink slip.

Notice that the clause set off by commas, *which everyone instinctively knows*, offers added information that we don't need to know to understand the sentence's main idea: There are certain unwritten laws in the workplace that can make you either a valued employee or one headed for a pink slip.

RESTRICTIVE AND NONRESTRICTIVE PHRASES

My teacher also mentioned restrictive and nonrestrictive phrases. Please explain.

Participial phrases introduce restrictive and nonrestrictive phrases in sentences. As stated in Chapter One, a participle is simply an action word (verb) that ends *ing*, *ed*, *t*, *en*, or *n*. (Some examples of verbs with these endings are: *howling*, *deserted*, *swept*, *broken*, and *torn*.) You'll recall that an action word with one of these endings signals the beginning of a participial phrase.

Consider this example:

Restrictive phrase (no comma): Anyone cutting classes will be sent to the office for detention.

In this sentence it's important to know that not just anyone will be sent to the office. Only those cutting classes will face the dauntless disciplinarian who doles out detentions. The phrase *cutting classes* restricts the meaning of the rest of the sentence, so the sentence doesn't need commas.

Here's an example of a nonrestrictive phrase:

Caleb, deserted by his girlfriend, learned that his beloved Hope had abandoned him because he had turned into a grammar geek.

In this sentence the fact that Caleb's girlfriend deserted him is added information because we're told this later in the sentence. Therefore, the phrase *deserted by his girlfriend* is nonrestrictive and needs commas.

The point that Caleb's girlfriend dropped him because he became a grammar geek is the main idea of this sentence. We use commas in this sentence to set off the extra information that we don't need.

To sum it up, like dependent clauses, participial phrases can also be restrictive and nonrestrictive. Now here's a quiz to see what you know about restrictive and nonrestrictive clauses and phrases.

QUICK QUIZ #9: RESTRICTIVE AND NONRESTRICTIVE CLAUSES AND PHRASES

Write your answers the same way that you did for the comma quiz. In the space before each sentence, write R for restrictive and NR for nonrestrictive. If the sentence is nonrestrictive, write a word you'd write before each comma. Remember that restrictive clauses and phrases do not need commas; nonrestrictive clauses and phrases do.

Score 10 points for each correct answer, which includes the type of clause or phrase, restrictive or nonrestrictive, and the correct punctuation. Find answers under Quick Quiz #9.

Hot Tip

- As you read each sentence, ask yourself whether the dependent clauses and participial phrases in each sentence restrict or change the meaning of the sentences. If they do, and the sentence wouldn't have the same impact without these clauses or phrases, then they are restrictive, and you won't use a comma.

  If, on the other hand, the clauses or phrases add information that isn't vital to the sentence's meaning or contain common knowledge, then they are nonrestrictive, and you will need a comma.

1. _____ The students anticipating a day off from school planned to build an igloo and ride snowmobiles.
2. _____ My boss leaning back in his chair fell with a loud crash to the floor.
3. _____ "University students who cut classes excessively will fail," the dean said at freshman orientation.
4. _____ Pablo who raises his hand to spell every word correctly hides an electronic spell-check in his backpack.
5. _____ Leah snoring loudly woke up her two roommates.
6. _____ The orders that our boss gave us looked impossible to carry out.
7. _____ My ESL teacher rewarded everyone who received an A in her class with a home-cooked dinner of Peking duck.
8. _____ The food at my favorite restaurant which is located in Parsippany is both delicious and reasonable.
9. _____ The elaborate ring engraved with the names of both partners cost Colin six paychecks.
10. _____ "All employees who write run-on sentences and misplaced modifiers will attend an after-hours grammar class," said the supervisor.

Now that you've mastered the comma, we'll move on to other punctuation marks you'll need to know.

Chapter Eight

The Rest of the Punctuation Marks

All You Need to Know

Why is it important to know about the semicolon, colon, italics, quotation marks, parentheses, dash, and apostrophe? Will anyone really care if I don't know how to use these pesky little punctuation marks?

Besides helping you feel in command when you write so that you know exactly when to add a dash, pop in parentheses, or highlight a thought with italics, knowing about these other marks of punctuation adds energy to your writing.

You can link thoughts with a semicolon; add zest with a dash; create an aside with parentheses; and do countless, exciting things with punctuation. Like good grammar, punctuation helps you connect with your reader, giving your writing personality and making it fun to read.

Knowing how to punctuate properly will help you whenever you write or speak. It helps put you in control.

They're good enough reasons for me! What else do I need to know about punctuation?

THE SEMICOLON

Let's start with the semicolon. Instead of joining independent clauses with a coordinating conjunction (*and*, *but*, *or*, *nor*, *for*, *yet*, or *so*), sometimes try using a semicolon in place of a conjunction. It's another way to write a compound sentence and to add variety to your writing.

Example: Today I went to a step-aerobics class for the first time; I'm not sure if I'll return because every bone and muscle throbbed.

In this sentence the semicolon takes the place of the conjunction *but*.

You'll also want to use a semicolon between parts of a sentence joined by the following words: *besides, accordingly, moreover, nevertheless, furthermore, otherwise, therefore, however, consequently, also, thus,* and *instead.* When you see these words, put a semicolon before them and a comma after.

Example: Talula tried to impress the judges of the drama contest; however, when she clumsily fell into the set, they asked her to leave.

You can also use a semicolon before the following expressions when they precede independent clauses: *for example, namely, that is, for instance, in fact,* and *on the contrary.* As with the previous group of words, use a comma after these expressions.

Example: James aced all the quizzes in this book; in fact, he decided to change his major from mortuary science to English.

Finally, you'll want to use a semicolon to separate the different ideas mentioned when a series contains commas within its elements. You can also use semicolons to avoid confusion if the items in a series are very long. This will help make your sentences easier to read than if you'd used commas alone.

Example: In our company we have these types of workers: the go-getter, who works through the night to get the job done; the pretender, who brags about imaginary accomplishments but does little work; and the loafer, who texts friends all day and knows all the latest gossip.

THE COLON

Okay. I understand how to use the semicolon. Now tell me about the colon. I already know it's used after a name in a business letter and in writing the time.

Here's another sentence using the colon in the same way that you saw it used in the previous sentence—before a list of items. It also shows how a list that's detailed, rather than short and simple, would use semicolons rather than commas to make the meaning clear. If a list contains short segments, use a comma.

Example: Haley's mother discovered the following items in her closet after she left home for college: a bologna sandwich that had mildewed; a rusty, old hamster cage; and an excuse note to her teacher, explaining how her mother had accidently lined the cage with her homework.

You can also use a colon before a long, formal statement.

Example: Tyrone's ex-girlfriend issued the following proclamation: "Don't call unless I call you first; don't date any of my friends; don't try to wiggle your way into my life again; and give me back the pricey presents I gave you."

Notice that we also used semicolons in this sentence between the different items because they were longer than usual.

ITALICS

I have a question about italics. I get confused about whether to underline or to use italics when I'm writing on the computer.
    Some teachers tell you to underline rather than use the italics font. However, today most people use italics. It's best to check with your teacher before deciding which to use. Also, consult the stylebook your teacher recommends, and choose to use one or the other, italics or underlining. Some teachers are very particular about which to use, so to be safe, abide by what they ask.
    Use italics or underlining to underline book titles, long poems, full-length plays, works of art (pictures, musical compositions, and statues), movies, names of newspapers, magazines, companies, and ships.
    If you're writing something that has an apostrophe followed by an *s*, you don't need to italicize the apostrophe and the *s*. (Notice the word *Today's* in the sentence below.)

Example (book title): Whenever I can't sleep, I read *Grammar Drills for Today's Student,* and within minutes I drift off.

When citing a magazine or newspaper title, don't italicize the words *a*, *an*, and *the* before a magazine or newspaper.

Example: When my teacher called on me, I was reading comics in the *Philadelphia Inquirer.*

Use italics for foreign words that you think most people don't know. If you think most people understand the words, or English-speaking people use them extensively and they're in the dictionary, then don't bother using italics. For example, you wouldn't italicize the word *champagne* since we use it all the time.

Example (foreign words): Our guests considered it a *faux pas* when Sweetie, our guinea pig, ate applesauce from a dish at our table.

Use italics for words referred to as words and letters referred to as letters.

Example (words referred to as words): The word *discombobulate* has five syllables and sounds a lot like what it means.

Example (letters referred to as letters): Mr. Diaz was so fussy that he'd deduct points from your grade if you forget to dot your *i*'s or cross your *t*'s. (Just italicize the letter you're referring to, not the apostrophe and the *s*.)

Some writers go overboard with italics by overusing them for emphasis. Use your judgment when italicizing words, and don't get carried away, or your reader may become distracted by too many italicized words.

QUOTATION MARKS

I sometimes have trouble with quotation marks. I'm not sure about how to handle interrupted quotations and whether other punctuation marks go inside or outside the quotation marks.
    Before we talk about interrupted quotes and whether to put punctuation inside or outside quotation marks, let's look at two different types of quotations, indirect and direct.

Indirect quotation: My friend said that whoever loses the Frisbee game will treat the winner to a sausage pizza and a movie.

Direct quotation: My friend said, "Whoever loses the Frisbee will treat the winner to a sausage pizza and a movie."

The indirect quotation gives us the information indirectly (with the use of *that*), while the direct quotation uses the friend's exact words.

Notice how the direct quotation is punctuated. A comma goes before the quote, and the quotation begins with a capital letter. The quotation ends with a period and quotation marks. An interrupted quotation is another type of quote that starts, either pauses or comes to a dead stop, and then continues. With an interrupted quotation, remember to use a lower-case letter when you continue the quotation and to put a comma after *said*. On the other hand, if the second part of a broken quotation is a new sentence, begin the second sentence with a capital letter.

Compare these two examples:

Interrupted quotation (continued quotation): "One day last week," the teacher said to the principal, "someone squirted glue in my lock, and we couldn't get into the classroom."

Interrupted quotation (new sentence): "Grammar is never boring for me," Melvin said. "Whenever I complete a lesson, I reward myself with a gooey, crunchy chocolate bar."

Now for your question about punctuation inside or outside the quotation marks: Always place commas and periods inside quotation marks and colons and semicolons outside quotation marks. Notice that in the next two sentences we use a colon instead of a comma to introduce the quotes. Do this when you quote longer sentences such as the ones below.

Example 1 (period inside quotation): The class president said: "The best moment of the senior prom came when Ms. Pristine, our math teacher who's been teaching for fifty years, danced The Chicken Dance with our class."

Example 2 (semicolon outside quotation): Tito said to María: "Please disregard my flabby muscles, my poor complexion, and my lack of popularity when you decide whether to go out with me"; she stared back at him in amazement.

Here's something else to consider about placing punctuation marks inside or outside quotations. When the material quoted is a question or an exclamation, place these punctuation marks inside the quotation marks. However, when the whole sentence is a question or an exclamation, place question marks and exclamation points outside the quotation marks.

Example (Only the material inside the quotation is a question. Place punctuation inside quotations.): "How did Ms. O'Mara react when you got an A on your grammar test?" asked Waldo.

Example (The whole sentence is a question. Place punctuation outside quotations.): Did the teacher really say, "Since all of you passed the tests, I won't give you homework for a month"?

Example (exclamation points inside the quotation marks): The manager said, "You've done such an amazing job, Carlos, that I'm taking off a week and putting you in charge!"

Example (exclamation points outside the quotation marks): I'd love it if my boss would say, "I'm taking off a week and putting you in charge"!

Speaking of exclamation points, is there a rule about how often you can use them? Whenever I see too many of them, I think the person's writing looks wild and out of control.

I can see that you're starting to get a feeling for how to use grammar to enhance your writing. You're right. Too many exclamation points (or dashes and parentheses, for that matter) can give your writing an amateurish look and distract your reader from getting the message you're trying to relay.

I'm curious about writing dialogue. I never know when to start a new paragraph and how to use quotation marks when there are two or more people talking.

All you need to do is start a new paragraph every time you change speakers. Here's an example:

"Class, my intention is not to bore you into oblivion," said Mr. Tedium, my senior English teacher, after he preached for an hour about the evils of sentence fragments.

"Then why do you spend so much time on something we could learn in fifteen minutes?" asked Carmella.

"Because I'm the captain, and I'm in charge of this ship," Mr. Tedium snapped, flipping open his yellowed notebook.

QUOTATION MARKS VERSUS ITALICS

I'd like to know about quotation marks versus italics. Do I use quotation marks or italics with articles, poems, and chapters of books?

Use quotation marks for titles of chapters, articles, and parts of books or magazines. Italicize the titles of long poems and poetry collections.

Example (book chapter): Chapter 1 of my friend Igor's book, "Zombies, Vampires, and other Undead Creatures," gave me horrific nightmares.

Example (article): My teacher recommended an article in the *New York Times*: "Is Texting Ruining Our Writing Skills?"

Example (poem): My mother wrote my final absence note after referring to Shel Silverstein's poem "Sick." (Notice this poem's title is short, so we use quotation marks.)

Example (long poem): *The Odyssey* relates the adventures of Odysseus on his journey home after Troy fell. (We use italics here because *The Odyssey* is a long poem.)

QUOTE WITHIN A QUOTE

I once heard my teacher talk about a quote within a quote. What's that about?

All it means is that you use single quotation marks when a speaker who's being quoted states another person's exact words. The other person's words are enclosed in single quotation marks. Sometimes you might want to mention a poem in a sentence that already has quotations. The poem, which is ordinarily surrounded by double quotation marks, now gets single quotation marks.

Always end your sentences with a double quotation mark.

Example (speaker is quoting another person): Brady said, "As I recall, my English teacher's exact words were: 'How can you not be entranced by the scintillating study of punctuation and faulty parallelism?'"

Example (short poem title as part of a quotation): Ms. Danbury, the cat lady, said: "For Kitty Cat's birthday I baked her a lobster cake and read her 'Cat Calls.'"

PARENTHESES

Now that I know about quotation marks, what do I have to know about using parentheses?

We've talked about how the comma can set off ideas that we add to a sentence when they aren't greatly important to the sentence meaning.

You can also use parentheses to set off ideas that are incidental or a little added information, but try not to use parentheses too often as they can intrude on the smooth flow of sentences and distract your reader. Use parentheses to set off a few words or a complete sentence. Look at these examples:

Example 1 (complete sentence): Byron always chose a smart girlfriend (his current one would not win awards for academics), but she could cook like a top chef, and that trumped brilliance for him.

Example 2 (a few words): I'm going shopping (discount and secondhand stores) and hope to come home with some exciting finds.

You don't need to start the first word in parentheses with a capital letter if the parentheses are inside the sentence. However, if the material in parentheses is a separate sentence, start with a capital. In this case, you'll need to end with a period inside the parentheses.

THE DASH

That was easier than I thought. Now bring on the dash!
We use the dash to show an important break in thought. The dash often serves the same function as parentheses but with more dramatic flair. In other words, the dash makes a stronger statement. As with parentheses, you can include parts of a sentence or a complete sentence.

Avoid using too many dashes as they can give your writing a jerky, abrupt sound.

Example: Miguel's English teacher gave him an ultimatum—Ms. Strident's harshness stunned him—start passing all tests or stay after school for tutoring every day.

You can also use the dash to mean *namely*, *in other words*, or *that is* and other expressions that come before explanations. In this case, you'll use only one dash.

Example: That party was the most boring I've ever attended—just as they did in junior high, the ladies congregated on one side of the room, and the men on the other.

In the sentence above, the dash takes the place of *in other words* or *that is*.

APOSTROPHES

Another thing I need to know about punctuation is how to use apostrophes. I'm not sure of when to put the apostrophe before or after the *s*.
Singular words using apostrophes to show possession will give you no problems.

Examples: clown, clown's; hair stylist, hair stylist's.

It's a little trickier if you're writing a plural possessive, but if you think about it, you'll be able to figure it out with no trouble.

Say you want to make the word *grandfather* possessive in both its singular and plural forms. First, think of how many grandfathers you're talking about. If it's one, add an *apostrophe s* (grandfather's) to make it plural.

However, if you're talking about a slew of grandfathers owning something, you'll first make the word plural (*grandfathers*) and then add an apostrophe.

Example: The grandfathers' bowling league from Chang's Emporium won every tournament.

Some people have problems with *its* versus *it's* when they're dealing with apostrophes. That's because we usually think of an apostrophe as letting us know someone owns something or is a part of it, as in *worker's* benefits or *neighbors'* houses.

Think of it as the opposite with its/it's. When you want to show possession, use *its* (no apostrophe). When you want to write a contraction (shorter form of the word) for *it is*, use *it's (apostrophe).*

Example (its): The robot clapped its hands to show that it enjoyed the movie. (shows possession)

Example (it's): It's not every day that Colin's teacher rewards him with a monster cookie. (contraction)

As you probably know, apostrophes are also used in contractions, such as can't (cannot), wouldn't (would not), shouldn't (should not).

When shouldn't I use apostrophes?
Good question—you knew there had to be some exceptions. For one thing, you shouldn't use apostrophes for capital letters and numbers.

Example: Lissett studied microbiology under two Ph.D.s.

On the other hand, here's a sentence using *Ph.D.* that calls for an apostrophe:

Gabe attended the Ph.D.s' award ceremonies.

In this sentence, there was more than one Ph.D., and we wanted to indicate possession. However, if Gabe attended only one award ceremony, we would say:

Gabe attended the Ph.D.'s award ceremony.

Example using dates: Don't use an apostrophe with dates: The 1920s were filled with excitement and daring social customs.

However, if you're referring to numbers and the sentence meaning needs clarification so that it doesn't sound confusing, use an apostrophe.

Example: Cross your t's if you want the teacher to think you took your time to proofread your work.

If you didn't use an apostrophe, the word *t's* would look like *ts* and wouldn't make sense. As you know by now, when you think about using good grammar, you're simply using good sense.

Now it's time for a quiz on other punctuation marks you've learned.

QUICK QUIZ #10: THE REST OF THE PUNCTUATION MARKS

This quiz includes the semicolon (S), colon (C), comma, (COM), italics (I) (use underlining for this quiz unless you're taking it on the computer), quotation marks (Q), interrupted quote (IQ), quote with a new sentence (QNS), question marks outside quotation marks (QO), exclamation points with quotations (E), parentheses (P), dash (D), and apostrophes (A). If the sentence is correct write C.

As you did before, write the word that comes before the punctuation. Then, using the abbreviations given above, write the name of each punctuation mark or marks you need in the sentence. Note that some sentences may have more than one error.

Use a separate line for each part of the answer so that you won't get confused when you check it with the answer key under Quick Quiz #10.

You must get all the punctuation right to gain all the points. Score 10 points for each correct sentence.

1. I went to see the counselor I asked if he'd talk to my English teacher about not counting my last test in my average. (Eliminate the run-on, but don't use a period.)
2. At the managers convention my boss did more eating and gossiping than setting policy. (Use possessive plural.)
3. Tyree and his friends kept a tally of how many times their science teacher said ah hum; it helped them stay awake.
4. When Quincy's teacher saw her reading the *New York Times*, her eyes widened in amazement.
5. I suddenly decided the decision still amazes me to stop writing run-ons and to become a grammar champ.
6. At our school we have the following types of students the slacker, who never studies, the apple polisher, who gives the teacher an apple every day, and the super-brain who knows the answer before the teacher asks.
7. Did Coach say, You're off the team if you fail one more test?
8. Shakira said that the production assistant's job didn't pay much but that it was exciting seeing her favorite stars perform in the movie.
9. "If you want to learn how to speak good English," the ESL teacher said it helps to watch the evening news, and if you want to learn slang and everyday conversation, watch talk shows.
10. Today we're having a pizza party and a movie Ms. Lee said you deserve some fun after revising your essays all afternoon.

You've done it! You know how to create a variety of sentences, and you know how to punctuate perfectly.

Later we'll get to what all this has been leading up to: how to write a dynamite essay on any topic, perfecting it with all the grammar and punctuation we've reviewed. But first we'll look at some grammatical problems that every writer faces.

Chapter Nine

Agreement Problems

How to Spot and Solve Them

What are some mistakes other than run-ons and sentence fragments that can make my writing look bad?

Along with run-on sentences and fragments, some errors stand out more than others under the scrutiny of your English teacher's red pen. Agreement errors often create problems for students, but if you remember the basic principle that **a subject must agree with its verb in number**, you'll never have trouble with agreement.

That sounds easy, but I sometimes wonder which verbs to use with prepositional phrases.

Remember to look for the subject of the sentence rather than at the object of the prepositional phrase. Of course there are exceptions, and we'll deal with them soon. However, most of the time, refer to the subject to figure out which verb to use. Here's an example:

My boss's uncanny knowledge about our private office conversations always astounds me.

The subject of the sentence is *knowledge,* which is singular in number. Therefore, use the verb *astounds,* which is also singular. Students who aren't grammar superstars like you might mistakenly think that the object of the preposition, *conversations*, which is plural, is the subject.

SINGULAR AND PLURAL PRONOUNS

I know that certain pronouns are singular and others are plural, but I don't know how to tell. I'm also not sure of which verbs to use with these pronouns.

Here are the singular pronouns, which take singular verbs: *each, either, neither, one, everyone, everybody, no one, nobody, anyone, anybody, someone,* and *somebody.*

Example: "Everyone *looks* sleepy," said Ms. Charisma as she explained subject-verb agreement. "I can't imagine why."

Since *everyone* is a singular pronoun, use *looks,* a singular verb. Substitute *he* or *she* (singular pronouns) for *everyone,* and you'll know you have to use a singular verb.

More traditional grammarians believe that *either* (when used with *or*) and *neither* (when used with *nor*) should always take singular verbs, especially in formal writing. Others believe that if you see two nouns in the sentence, one singular and one plural, you should let the noun closest to the word *either* or *neither* determine whether you use a singular or plural verb. You'll find two examples later in this chapter.

I've always wondered about this: I thought that an *s* on the end of a word, in this case, *looks,* means that the verb is plural. You said that *everyone* needs a singular verb.

An *s* does mean that a *noun* is plural, but singular verbs often have an *s* ending. Again, substitute the word *he* or *she* for *everyone,* and you'll come up with the answer he or she *looks* (singular verb).

Use your good sense in determining which type of verb to use. In this book and in the quiz that follows, we'll use a plural verb if it's closest to *either* or *neither.* However, always abide by your teacher's rules in this and other grammar questions.

Here are two sentences using *either* with a plural verb.

Example 1: Either the college president or administrators determine if a student will graduate. Use *determine,* a plural verb, because it is near *administrators,* a plural noun.

Example 2: "Either the principal or some teachers are going with me to the English awards dinner," Wilbur said to his unimpressed classmates. Use *are,* a plural verb, because it is near *teachers,* a plural noun.

On the other hand, if you're using *either* or *neither* followed by a prepositional phrase and a plural noun, most grammar buffs would advise you to use a singular verb. In this case, *either* means *either one* and *neither* means *neither one*.

Example 1: Neither of the cut-off jeans *is* suitable for the opera.

Example 2: "Either of the nurses *is* ready to give you the injection," the doctor said, smiling.

I understand about singular verbs. Now tell me which pronouns usually take plural verbs.
   Several, few, both, and *many* take plural verbs.

Example: *Many* study grammar but sometimes aren't sure about how to apply it to writing.

If you substitute the plural pronoun *they* for many, you'll know that you should use the verb *study*.
   When followed by a prepositional phrase, *some, any, none, all*, and *most* may be either plural or singular depending upon the sentence meaning. For a good clue about whether to use a singular or plural verb, look at the phrase following it. Here are two examples:

Example (plural verb): "*Some* of your answers were brilliant," said Professor Ramirez. (Substitute the pronoun *them* for *your answers*, and you'll know the answer is *were*, a plural verb.)

Example (singular verb): "*None* of the food was edible," Myra said to the caterer, who had spent hours preparing it.

Substitute the pronoun *it* (singular) for *food*, and you'll get the answer, *was*, a singular verb.

COMPOUND SUBJECTS

Tell me about compound subjects joined by *and*. I always wonder whether to use a singular or plural verb.
   Usually compound subjects take a plural verb, but if the subjects are thought of as one unit, they take a singular verb.

Example (compound subject with a plural verb): "The beginning and the end of your essay *are* well-written, but the middle bores and confuses me," Professor Fastidious said, arching her eyebrow.

In this sentence *beginning* and *end* are the compound subjects of the sentence, so use the plural verb *are*. Test it by substituting *they* for *beginning and end*.

Example (compound subject with a singular verb): Bagels and lox is a delicious breakfast.

In this sentence *bagels and lox* is thought of as one thing, so it's considered singular and takes the singular verb *is*.

Can you think of other compound subjects thought of as a single unit? Here are a few: *bacon and eggs*, *bread and butter*, and *stress and strain*. You'll remember to use a singular verb if you substitute the pronoun *it* for the compound subject and write: *It is a delicious breakfast.*

QUICK QUIZ #11: AGREEMENT

See if you can spot the mistakes in the following ten sentences. Correct the verbs in these sentences. If you think the italicized verb is the wrong verb, correct it; if it's correct, write a C. Find the answer key under Quick Quiz #11. Score 10 points for each correct answer.

1. The beginning and the end of the school year *is* the most fun.
2. Tossing and turning all night *are* my usual sleep pattern before a killer test.
3. If everyone *makes* a promise to study for the final, Mr. Silver promises to bake five hand-tossed pepperoni pizzas for the class.
4. *Have* either Towanda or Keith ever tasted Moo Goo Gai Pan?
5. Mr. Brainchild's knowledge of exciting teaching methods *have* endeared him to his students.
6. Most of the fruit *were* fresh.
7. Either the teacher or the counselors *is* likely to call parents if their children miss too many days of school.
8. One of my lucky friends *has* been awarded "Best Grammar Student of the Year" award, which entitles him to a library of grammar books and a "Grammar Rules" T-shirt.
9. None of the students *likes* a long school day.
10. Hot dogs and baked beans *are* standard lunch fare at the company cafeteria.

INCLUSIVE LANGUAGE

Here's another question I have about pronouns. My boss always talks about not using sexist or noninclusive language in the mail we send out. Wouldn't it sound too wordy to use *his* or *her* instead of simply using one word—*his*? How can I use noninclusive language and still make my writing sound good?

Here's the type of sentence you're talking about:

Each of the students signed a contract with his English teacher stating that he would study grammar for an hour each night.

What's wrong with using *his* and *he* in this sentence? It's an easy solution and gets the point across. The only problem is that it leaves out half the population, the same way it does if we use words like *mailman, fireman, policeman,* and *businessman.* Wouldn't it sound more accurate if we called them *mail carriers, firefighters, police officers,* and *business people* since both men and women fill these jobs? We call using nonsexist pronouns and terms to describe people *inclusive language* because we want to include the entire population when we're writing and speaking.

Here's one way to solve the problem posed in the example above: You may want to substitute *his* or *her* or *he* and *she* for *his* and *he.*

Doesn't that sound worse than using *his* and *he*?
It may sound wordy to some people, but as we continue to explore alternatives to sexist language, we'll probably think of more possibilities. Maybe you'd feel more comfortable using *he* in some sentences and *she* in others; in other words, alternate their use evenly throughout your writing. Whatever you decide, it helps to be aware of how we can use the language to include both sexes.

Is there anything else I can do to make my language inclusive?
Sometimes making the entire sentence plural will work well.

Example: The students signed a contract with their English teacher stating that they would study grammar for an hour each night.

Here's another question related to using inclusive language. What do you think of using *their* to refer to the pronoun *everyone*? Here's a sentence:
Everyone gave their word that they would stay in and study instead of going trick-or-treating.

It isn't correct to use *their* in this case. Even though many people do it, it's still not a good idea to use it. It's best not to use *their*, which is plural, with *everyone*, which is a singular pronoun. Instead, you may want to make the subject of the sentence plural, so that the entire sentence is plural. *His or her word* would probably sound awkward to most people.

Example (using *students*, a plural subject): The *students* gave their word that they would stay in and study instead of going trick-or-treating.

On the other hand, if the people you're writing about are one sex, you can use the pronoun referring to that sex and forget about using *his/her* and *he/she*.

Example 1: Everyone gave *his* word that *he* would stay in and study instead of going trick-or-treating.

Example 2: Everyone gave *her* word that *she* would stay in and study instead of going trick-or-treating.

QUICK QUIZ #12: USING INCLUSIVE LANGUAGE

Here's a quick quiz (just five sentences) on using inclusive language. Change each sentence any way you want to make it inclusive of both sexes. Score 20 points for each correct answer, or note the number you got right out of five questions at the top of your paper.

1. Each student packed a lunch for his trip to the zoo.
2. Everyone in the office pooled her resources to buy a shower gift for the newlyweds.
3. The mailman delivered a notice to my house, saying that I'd won the sweepstakes.
4. An employee will receive a bonus if he reaches a high quota in computer sales.
5. Firemen worked diligently to stop the raging flames.

PRONOUN CASE

It's sometimes hard to figure out which pronoun to use. The pronouns I use sound okay to me, but they often end up being wrong. Sometimes it's hard deciding whether to use *him and me* or *he and I* . Another problem comes up when one object is a noun and one is a pronoun. I don't always know which pronoun is right.

Before we begin to look at some challenging examples of using pronouns, we'll review nominative and objective case. We discussed subjects and objects earlier in this book (Chapter Two), so understanding nominative and objective case will be easy for you.

A pronoun used as the subject of a sentence is in the nominative case. Remember: To find the subject, ask *who* or *what* before the action word (predicate). If a noun or pronoun follows a linking verb, it's also in the nominative case. Here are the nominative forms: *I, you, he, she, it, we,* **and** ***they.***

Study these two sentences using pronouns in the nominative case:

Example 1: "*She* and *I* are the perfect couple," said Jason. "We love to bungee jump, eat sushi, and walk in the rain."

She, I, and *we* are subjects of the verb *are*; therefore, they're in the nominative case.

Example 2: It was I who told the doctor that the fish oil tablets he prescribed made me smell like a dead mackerel.

I follows the linking verb *was* and is called a predicate nominative; it is in the nominative case.

If you think it sounds stuffy to say *It was I*—and a lot of people do—you can eliminate the first two words of the sentence and say *I told the doctor*. Good English doesn't have to sound forced or affected. You can be yourself and still sound grammatically correct.

Before we discuss your question about which pronouns to use in objective case, we'll briefly review objective case, which you learned about in Chapter Two.

Objective case describes a pronoun used as a direct object, indirect object, or object of a preposition. Remember that to find the subject of a sentence, we ask *who* or *what* before the verb. To find the object of a sentence, just reverse the process, and ask *whom* or *what* after the verb. To find the indirect object of a sentence, ask *to* or *for whom* or *what* after the verb.

So now we're back to my original question: What happens if you have two objects, a pronoun being one of them, after the preposition? Sometimes I'm not sure about when to use *I* or *me*.

You're talking about a compound object after a preposition. Here's a sentence just like that, this time using objects of the preposition.

Aunt Millie baked a cherry pie for Dexter and me.

If you see a sentence like this one and you aren't sure of which pronoun to use, eliminate the first object of the preposition (in this case, *Dexter*), and see which pronoun would sound better after the preposition. In this instance, you'd come up with *baked a cherry pie for me* because *baked a cherry pie for I* wouldn't sound right.

Here's another example of a prepositional phrase, this time with two pronouns:

School has been fun for her and me this year. (*Her* and *me* are objects of the preposition *for*. Again, test each pronoun separately before deciding on your answer.)

But that doesn't sound right!
    You're not alone in saying that. To many people it doesn't. Maybe that's because a lot of people use the wrong pronouns. If you understand the reasons behind the answers and how to test for them, coming up with the right pronouns will get easier.

Here's another sentence that sounds right to me, but I suspect it's wrong:

The boss gave my coworker and I a bonus for selling the most thermal underwear.

Wouldn't it sound uneducated to say my coworker and *me*?
    In this sentence the right pronoun to use is *me*. The answer is *me* because *me* is in the objective case. *Coworker* and *me* are the indirect objects of the verb *gave*.

Let's practice using our test again to see which pronoun you think is right.

My boss gave my coworker and (*me* or *I*) a bonus for selling the most thermal underwear.

My boss gave *me* a bonus for selling the most thermal underwear. (indirect object, *me*)

How do you think it would sound if you said, "My boss gave *I* a bonus . . ."? You be the judge. When you break down the compound objects like this into two separate sentences, you'll have no trouble finding the right answer.

Here's another example using a compound object of the preposition:

People in the office heard the disagreement between my boss and *me*.

Me is the only answer here because it's the object of the preposition *between*. *I* can never be an object pronoun. It may sound better to some people to say *I*, but isn't it better to sound wrong and be right?

INCOMPLETE CONSTRUCTION

Are there any other mistakes I should avoid that deal with the case of pronouns?

Sometimes when a sentence isn't played out to its logical conclusion, you have what's called an incomplete construction, and you may wonder which pronoun to use. Let's look at a couple of examples and see which answer you'd choose:

Lauren is more intrigued by the study of grammar than (I/me).

If you thought about which words you'd need to complete this sentence, you'd add *am* after *than I*. In other words, mentally complete the sentence to know which pronoun to use. In this case, *I* is the subject of the clause *than I am*. Here's another sentence using an incomplete construction:

Mr. Stickler gave Cody a better grade than (I/me).

Again, if you added the implied words to the sentence, you'd say *a better grade than he gave me.*

Sometimes, incomplete constructions can imply different ideas, depending on the pronoun used.

Example: Dad praises you more than *me*. (Meaning: Dad praises you more than he praises me.)

Example: Dad praises you more than *I*. (Meaning: Dad praises you more than I do.)

QUICK QUIZ #13: PRONOUNS

Now it's time to test your knowledge of pronouns. Correct the pronouns that need it by writing only the part of the sentence that needs correcting. Write C if the italicized pronouns are used correctly. Add or leave out words if it will make the sentence sound better. Score 10 points for each correct answer. Look for answers in the back of the book under Quick Quiz #13.

1. My boyfriend's mother baked a pheasant for *he and I*.
2. Mr. Ogelsby gave Sara a better recommendation than *me*. (Explain what the sentence means. What words did you fill in?)
3. My friend is more interested in sports than *I*.
4. When the dean told *she and I* to report to the office, we expected a pat on the back, not a slap on the wrist.
5. My hairdresser created a new look for Andy and *I*; we emerged from the shop looking like Frankenstein and his bride.
6. It was *me* who called you at 3:00 a.m. to ask if you had anything good in your house to eat.
7. Because we were her best customers, the baker gave *my friend* and *me* a free sample of every cookie in her shop.
8. My *coworker and me* use our lunch hour to burn off calories by walking.
9. My ESL teacher helps my family and *I* learn English.
10. The only two people who attended the seminar were *my friend and I*.

Chapter Ten

Words Often Confused

How to Get Them Straight

Here's something else I'd like to ask about: words people often confuse. For instance, I'm not sure about when you should use *awhile* or *a while* and when you should use *which* or *that*.

That's a good question and something everyone wants to know. Sometimes a simple mistake using these words can mark a writer as an amateur, so it's important to be aware of the differences in meaning in these similarly spelled or sounding words.

Words that people confuse come in many different forms: some are homonyms, words that sound alike but have different meanings, such as *to*, *too*, and *two*; some are words that sound similar like *moral* and *morale* but have different meanings; and some are words that simply give people trouble because they're not sure of how to use them, such as *appraise* and *apprise*.

Here's a list of words that people frequently confuse.

WORDS OFTEN CONFUSED

1. **Advice, advise:** *Advice* (noun) is guidance you give someone. *Advise* (verb) is to give that advice.

    Example:

    Evan's dad was always giving him *advice,* but whenever he'd *advise* him, his son would do the opposite.

2. **All ready, already:** *All ready* means prepared or everyone is ready. *Already* means previously or by this time.

    Examples:

    I was *all ready* to go to the hockey game when a wicked cold landed me in bed.

    I was happy to learn that the guests had *already* eaten the roasted pig by the time I arrived.

3. **Affect, effect:** *Affect* (verb) means to influence. When used as a noun it can mean an emotional state and is often used by psychologists. *Effect* is the result or consequence of something when it's used as a noun. As a verb, it can mean to accomplish, but we don't use this definition of the word too often. (See the last example for *effect* used as a verb.)

    Examples:

    The mildew in the old house *affected* me badly. (verb)

    Carter's *affect* often upsets his colleagues because he acts super-ior and surly. (noun)

    We felt the *effects* of the blizzard for weeks to come. (noun)

    The mayor has *effected* changes that have caused the town to go bankrupt. (verb)

4. **All right:** Don't spell it *alright* since *all right* is all right!

    Example:

    "No, it's not all right if you eat a bag of corn chips and two donuts before dinner," Mom said to her pleading son.

5. **All together, altogether**: *All together* means everyone or everything is in the same place. *Altogether* means entirely.

   Examples:

   When we were *all together* at the family reunion in Georgia, Zane proposed to Tara.

   The editor was *altogether* wrong when she rejected that novel; it went on to become a best seller.

6. **A lot**: *A lot* is always two words, never one.

   Example:

   Because *a lot* of people like the taste of salt, many soup manufacturers load their products with sodium.

7. **Allusion, illusion**: An *allusion* is a reference to something. An *illusion* is a false perception.

   Examples:

   Shakespeare made an *allusion* to a Greek tragedy that baffled most students.

   The magician created an *illusion* that stumped us all when she was able to escape from a car submerged in the ocean.

8. **Appraise, apprise**: *Appraise* means give a price or value to something. To *apprise* is to tell someone about a situation.

   Examples:

   A lot of people want to have their gold *appraised* to gain extra money.

   Chase's boss will *apprise* him of the merger with a rival company if he promises to keep it in confidence.

9. **A while, awhile**: *A while* is an amount of time that's undetermined. *Awhile* means for a while or for a time.

   Examples:

   The ban on texting while driving has been in effect for *a while.*

   The teacher's lecture on misplaced modifiers lasted *awhile,* and we couldn't wait for it to end.

10. **Between, among**: *Between* relates to two people while *among* relates to a group of three of more.

    Examples:

    ***Between* you and me, I'm going to look for a more interesting job.**

    The disagreement *among* the three siblings resolved itself when their mother threatened to cut off their allowance.

11. **Break, brake**: *Break* means to destroy, while *brake* is the stopping device on your car.

    Examples:

    "Don't *break* your leg when you go skiing," Donna's mother warned her before her honeymoon.

    It's important to use your emergency *brake* when your regular brakes fail.

12. **Breath, breathe**: *Breath* is a noun meaning the air you inhale or exhale, while *breathe* is a verb meaning you're taking a breath.

    Examples:

    Being aware of your *breath* can help you relax.

    When we *breathe,* we're rarely aware of our *breath.*

13. **Capital, capitol**: *Capital* means the main city of a town or region, or money. *Capitol* is the building or statehouse

   Examples:

   The child prodigy knew all the state *capitals*.

   The private school raised enough *capital* from the alumni to keep it running another year.

   The state *capitol* is the scene for many government functions.

14. **Choose, chose**: *Choose* means to select. *Chose* is the past tense of choose.

   Examples:

   Malik was grateful that he could *choose* his college professors.

   Irina *chose* an elegant silk dress for her wedding.

15. **Coarse, course**: Coarse means loose or rough in texture or crude. Course means the path of action or travel or a course you're studying.

   Examples:

   Angel's hair was so *coarse* that she couldn't get a brush through it.

   Some theater goers were so offended by the *coarse* words in the play that they walked out.

   The plane went off *course* because of the driving storm.

   Many students take the academic *course* because they want to attend college.

16. **Complement, compliment**: As a noun, *complement* means something that completes, while as a verb it means to complete. When people give *compliments*, they're giving praise.

Examples:

The airy white wicker furniture presents a *complement* **to the coziness of the beach house.**

The light dessert of lemon mousse *complemented* **the rich, heavy main course of filet gorgonzola.**

When someone *compliments* **her, Ali smiles graciously and says, "Thank you."**

17. **Council, counsel**: *Council* is a group that advises or gathers to accomplish something. *Counsel* used as a noun is advice, and *counsel* used as a verb means to give advice.

    Examples:

    Members of the city *council* **discussed the advisability of a curfew on school nights.**

    The warring couple accepted their friends' *counsel* **and reconciled.**

    It's easy to *counsel* **other people, but it's sometimes hard to** *counsel* **yourself.**

18. **Desert, Desert, dessert**: A *desert* is an arid or dry region. *Desert* means to leave. You eat *dessert* after a meal.

    Examples:

    After stomping through the *desert,* **the hiking party was happy to see the rescue team.**

    After the man *deserted* **his wife, she started a new life.**

    We were too full after the elaborate dinner to eat *dessert.*

19. **Disinterested, uninterested**: *Disinterested* means that someone is impartial, while *uninterested* mean you're not interested in something.

Examples:

The principal was fair in solving disputes as she appeared *disinterested* when both parties presented their cases.

When her employer brought out charts and graphs to make his point, Tamika appeared *uninterested.*

20. **Elicit, illicit:** *Elicit* means to bring out something, while *illicit* means illegal.

Examples:

The professor always *elicits* a response from our Spanish literature class because of her dynamic teaching methods.

Because of her *illicit* activities, the public official went to prison.

21. **Farther, further:** *Farther* refers to measurable distances. *Further* relates to abstract differences or something you can't measure.

Examples:

Jeremy's friends live *farther* from him than they did in high school.

Indira's children are *further* ahead of her in their knowledge of computers.

22. **Fewer, less:** *Fewer* refers to a specific number or one you can measure or count and *less* refers to an unspecific amount.

Examples:

Tristan got *fewer* clients for his snowplowing business during the warm winter.

Many people find themselves with *less* money before they get their next paychecks.

23. **Formally, formerly:** *Formally* means properly, according to the rules, while *formerly* means back then, in the past.

Examples:

In days gone by, people behaved more *formally* in social situations.

The president of our company was *formerly* a circus performer.

24. **Ingenious, ingenuous**: *Ingenious* means clever and skillful, while *ingenuous* means naive, innocent, or frank.

Examples:

Ryan's *ingenious* method of helping people save money on fuel oil made him a millionaire.

Although Lily was an *ingenuous* young lady, she sensed when people tried to take advantage of her good nature.

25. **Its, it's**: *Its* is the possessive form of it. *It's* is the contraction for it is.

Examples:

The dog always washed *its* paws before he ate.

It's a known fact that if you keep trying you'll eventually succeed.

26. **Lead, led, lead**: *Lead* is the present tense for go first or guide. *Led* is the past tense of lead. *Lead* is also a heavy metal and the graphite contained in a pencil.

Examples:

"*Lead* me to the buffet table," was the first thing Colton said when he arrived at the party.

The mother bear *led* her cubs to safety.

Zooey's legs felt as heavy as *lead* as she trudged through the swamplands.

27. **Lie, lay**: *Lie* (verb) means to rest or lie down. *Lie* (noun) means an untruth. The past tense of *lie* (verb) is *lay* and the past participle is *has/have lain*. *Lay* means to put an object down. *Laid* is the past tense of lay. *Has/have laid* is the past participle.

    Examples:

    Many people like to *lie* down for a nap after work. (present tense of *lie*)

    Luís *lay* down and watched TV when he got home from school. (past tense of *lie*)

    The children *have lain* down for a nap every day at preschool after they eat lunch. (past participle)

    Please *lay* the mail on the table. (present tense of lay)

    I *laid* your love letter on the bureau, but I swear I didn't read it. (past tense of *lay*)

    Ashley *has laid* her books on the kitchen table so that she can do her homework. (past participle of *lay*)

28. **Loose, lose**: *Loose* means not too tight, while *lose* means to experience the loss of.

    Examples:

    Emma's dress was so *loose* that she knew she'd finally lost weight.

    Aiden hates to *lose* at any game he plays.

29. **Moral, morale**: *Moral* means good or having virtue. It also means a lesson you learn from a story. *Morale* means a positive emotional or mental condition.

    Examples:

    Alaina has such high *moral* principles that her teachers recommended her for the citizenship award.

The theme of a story contains its lesson or *moral.*

The basketball coach prided himself in boosting his team's *morale.*

30. **Passed, past**: *Passed*, to go by or to pass a course, is the past tense of *pass.* You can use past as a noun, adjective, preposition, or adverb.

Examples:

Ian *passed* a deli on the way to work and stopped for a corned beef sandwich.

It's an accomplishment to *pass* all your subjects.

The *past* often appears better than the present. (noun)

The *past* president of the company made it what it is today. (adjective)

I could never drive *past* the Starlight Diner without going in for hot chocolate slathered with whipped cream. (preposition)

As I dived under water, a gigantic fish swam *past.* (adverb)

31. **Principal, principle**: The *principal* is the head of a school. *Principal* as an adjective can also mean the most important. *Principle* is a rule we live by; it is also a law or fact.

Examples:

An effective *principal* needs to get along with children, parents, and teachers.

Alyssa got a *principal* role in the play, and she spent long hours rehearsing.

My boss is a woman of *principle*; she listens to all sides of the story before making a decision.

If you study the *principles* of grammar, your writing powers will soar.

32. **Quiet, quite**: *Quiet* means still or silent, while *quite* means completely or entirely.

   Examples:

   Her husband was so *quiet* that her friends wondered if they bored him.

   Andre and Seamus are *quite* the basketball players.

33. **Stationary, stationery**: *Stationary* means not moving. *Stationery* means writing material, mainly paper.

   Examples:

   The car remained *stationary* after I put my foot on the gas pedal.

   These days few people write letters on fancy *stationery*.

34. **Which, that**: If the clause is restrictive (important to the sentence), use *that*. If not, use *which*.

   Examples:

   ***Jonathan Livingston Seagull*, *which* was rejected by many publishers, became a best seller. (The clause beginning with *which* is nonrestrictive because it is not vital to the sentence meaning.)**

   The school principal replaced all the desks *that* had graffiti on them. (The clause beginning with *that* is restrictive because it's important to the sentence meaning. If we used *which*, didn't use *that*, and inserted a comma, we'd be implying that the principal replaced *all* the desks, not just the ones with graffiti.)

35. **Their, there, they're**: *Their* is the possessive form of they. *There* means at that place, and *they're* is the contraction for they are.

   Examples:

   ***Their* cooking skills were so poor that they ordered takeout every night.**

There is the sapphire ring that looks like the evening sky in May.

They're going to the mountains to ski.

36. **To, too, two:** *To* is a preposition. *Too* means also and more than enough. *Two* indicates the number.

    Examples:

    Jonathan is taking a plane *to* his friend's house in Timbuktu.

    You're welcome to come to the barn raising *too*.

    Jumping in the ocean in cold weather is *too* much for me.

    Skylar said the subfreezing temperatures in the north were *too* much to bear.

    Irv can make *two* kinds of ice cream sodas.

37. **Waist, waste:** *Waist* is the middle part of your body, while *waste* is frivolous spending, or unused or useless things.

    Examples:

    When her clothes get too tight around the *waist*, Chloe goes on a diet.

    Todd's mother told him not to *waste* his money on his train collection.

    To avoid having too much *waste*, the chef donated the leftover food to charity.

38. **Weak, week:** *Weak* means lacking strength, while a *week* is seven days.

    Examples:

    Lamar felt *weak* after the football scrimmage.

    The interviewer told Emma that she'd know in a *week* if she got the job.

39. **Weather, whether**: *Weather* refers to the conditions outside, while *whether* shows doubt or a choice between alternatives.

Examples:

The *weather* was so pleasant that we decided to extend our stay in Palm Beach, Florida.

Shayna couldn't decide *whether* to travel to France or to Ireland.

40. **Who's, Whose**: *Who's* is a contraction for *who is*, while *whose* is a possessive pronoun.

Examples:

"*Who's* coming to the staff party, and what are you bringing?" my nosy coworker asked.

"I am the one *whose* phone you accidentally dialed at 4:00 a.m.," said Jayne's irate teacher.

41. **Your, you're**: *Your* is a possessive pronoun, and *you're* is a contraction for *you are*.

Examples:

Your facial expression often reveals what your words do not.

"Be sure *you're* bundled up; it's cold outside," the mother told her senior-citizen son.

QUICK QUIZ #14: WORDS OFTEN CONFUSED

Here's a quiz on words that are often confused. See how you do! This time you'll choose the word that best fits the sentence. Write the letter of the word you choose. Score 5 points for each correct answer.

1. The guests had (a) all ready (b) already eaten the cake when we arrived at the party.
2. The drone of the dental drill (a) affected (b) effected Kayla's nerves.

3. Maura felt sad after her divorce, but she feels (a) all right (b) alright now.
4. Many people thought the jury was (a) all together (b) altogether wrong when they let the defendant go free.
5. (a) A lot (b) Alot of people will vote in the next election.
6. Bernie was able to create the (a) illusion (b) allusion of being a good student, but he often copied his friend's homework.
7. Jill's friend (a) appraised (b) apprised her of the fact that her boyfriend was cheating.
8. Hopefully, snow won't hit our town for (a) awhile (b) a while.
9. The play's (a) coarse (b) course language bothered some people in the audience.
10. Rajon's striped tie (a) complimented (b) complemented his charcoal gray suit.
11. Because Milo was (a) disinterested (b) uninterested in science, he rarely did his homework.
12. Everyone thinks of Sofia as an (a) ingenuous (b) ingenious person because she seems naive about so many things.
13. The cat licked (a) it's (b) its chops whenever he saw me open a can of shrimp.
14. Although there are (a) fewer (b) less single people available in his age group, Marvin always manages to find a date.
15. Nima (a) laid (b) lay down for a nap after a grueling day of classes.
16. I (a) lied (b) laid my coat on the chair, but it was missing when I returned to my seat.
17. When people have (a) principals (b) principles, they strive to do the right thing.
18. (a) They're (b) Their hurrying to the party before the guests eat all the sour beef and dumplings.
19. The students (a) that (b) which the teacher singled out for hiding a whoopie cushion on her chair must stay after school.
20. Chanté attracted (a) less (b) fewer customers for her jewelry business when she raised her prices.

Chapter Eleven

Writing Style

What It Is and How to Get It

Now that I'm beginning to understand the nuts and bolts of grammar, I'd like to learn more about writing style. How can I make my individual style shine through in my writing?

You'll want to make your writing style uniquely your own, and there are a few things you can work on to help you discover your own writing style.

For one thing, it's important to sound like yourself and not to sound forced and artificial, which sometimes happens when students try to show off by using big, pretentious words they wouldn't ordinarily use or by rambling on about something they could say clearly and simply.

What techniques can you give me to help me say what I want to say so that people will listen without my sounding like I'm trying too hard to make an impression?

WORDINESS

One thing you can do is avoid wordiness, sometimes called *deadwood.* When you take too long to express your thoughts, it makes your reader want to shout, "What exactly is your point?"

Picture your English teacher, surrounded by 150 papers to mark, finding a sentence that reads like this:

**Shakespeare was able to write for his own generations and the genera-
tions to come, finding the common thread that unites all people in all
times and writing about it as no one else could.**

Try paring down this wordy sentence into one that helps readers instantly
connect with what the writer wants them to know:

**Shakespeare wrote in a unique style about universal themes that are as
relevant today as they were during Elizabethan times.**

CLICHÉS

**My teacher says I use too many clichés in my writing. What are they,
and what can I do to avoid them?**
    Clichés or trite expressions (of the "early bird catches the worm"/"what-
ever goes around comes around" variety) make your writing produce yawns.
And you know how contagious they are. You don't have to think to churn out
these lackluster expressions. Your teacher and everyone else will quickly
tune you out if you "take the easy way out."

JARGON

Along these lines, do your best to avoid jargon, another name for special
wording used by different professions. (Maybe you've heard your teacher
refer to a classmate as an "underachiever" rather than as someone who
doesn't work up to capacity). Jargon often muddles meaning because it
sounds technical and obscure.
    Here's an example of medical jargon, which is fine if you're working at
your local hospital or auditioning for a medical show:

**Transport the patient to the operating room stat because he's having a
myocardial infarction.** (jargon)

**Take the patient to surgery immediately because he's having a heart
attack.** (jargon free)

There are many other types of jargon: scientific, educational, and business,
for example. When you write research papers, you'll see many examples in
the sources you investigate. When you use your own words instead of jargon,
your writing sounds more natural.

EUPHEMISMS

When I was a kid and my uncle Mortimer died, everyone told me he had "passed away." I pictured him floating up on a cloud to the great beyond. When I asked Mom why they used that expression, she said, "It sounds better than *died* because it cushions the pain of death for his loved ones." Do you agree?

Although euphemisms (sugar-coated words) sometimes help us avoid fights, embarrassment, and, in the example you mentioned, pain, when we speak or write, it's best to avoid these expressions.

We often use euphemisms in our speech and writing. On the surface, they appear to be less offensive ways of saying what we really mean. Some examples are: *big boned* for overweight, *job action* for strike or work slowdown, *correctional facility* for prison, and *unmotivated* for lazy.

We also love to dream up fancy-sounding names for our jobs or what's wrong with us, like *sanitation engineer* for trash collector and *mechanically challenged* for someone who doesn't know how to fix things.

Euphemisms often cover up what we're really trying to say. Think before you use euphemisms. Like clichés, they're often the first thing that comes to mind, making writing boring and predictable.

NONSTANDARD ENGLISH

I once asked my English teacher why I shouldn't say *ain't*. I hear a lot of people using it, so what's the problem? I know it doesn't sound like great English, but it is in the dictionary. She said, "If you want to sound like an ignoramus, keep on using it."

It's true that the dictionary contains some words that could make you sound unintelligent when you speak or write. In addition to all the words we use in standard English, the dictionary contains colloquial expressions (slang) and some nonstandard expressions. Most people would agree that *ain't* fits into the nonstandard category, the worst kind of English you can use.

Unfortunately, people often brand you by the vocabulary you use, so it's best to use standard English (the words that educated people prefer using), at least in writing. Of course, everyone uses colloquial expressions or slang when talking informally to friends, but it's important to use standard English when you're speaking or writing in a formal situation, such as the classroom or workplace. If you're trying to improve your writing style, strive to avoid using nonstandard English.

No offense, but I've noticed that you've sometimes used slang in this book (for example, the subtitle of Chapter Three is "Big-Time Blunders Corrected"). Isn't this a double standard?

You're right. I've used slang throughout this book to help get my point across. Slang is part of the style of this book just as it may become part of your style when you write creatively or if you're trying to grab people's attention or sell them something.

However, when answering test questions, speaking in class, and writing business correspondence, it's best to stay away from slang—unless your teacher says you can use it.

ENDING A SENTENCE WITH A PREPOSITION

A lot of people say it's not a good idea to end a sentence with a preposition. But sometimes if you don't, the sentence sounds strange, as in: *About what did you complain?* instead of *What did you complain about?*

In many cases, it's not a good idea to end a sentence with a preposition. However, in the sentence you used and in other cases that sound right to you intuitively, it's perfectly acceptable. Here are two examples of ending a sentence with a preposition that you wouldn't want to use:

Where's the jam session *at?*
It's better to say: *Where's the jam session?* The word *at* serves no purpose in this sentence.

Where are you going *to?*
Say *Where are you going?* You don't need the *to.*

Whenever you're thinking about whether it's okay to end a sentence with a preposition, ask yourself how it sounds to end the sentence this way. Think about how the sentence would sound if you *didn't* end it with a preposition as in this example from a famous president.

Winston Churchill, the prime minister of Britain during World War II, supposedly said: "That is the sort of thing up with which I will not put!" to make fun of someone who had attacked him for ending a sentence with a preposition.

If the sentence read, "That is the sort of thing I will not put up with," the meaning would be clearer. Even though the grammar squad might pounce all over you, you'd connect better with your readers.

FAULTY PARALLELISM

Another problem that I think deals with writing style is what my teacher called faulty parallelism. He wrote it on my paper once, and I never did find out what it meant.

Faulty parallelism is a fancy term for what happens when you suddenly change the types of words or phrases you're using in a sentence. And, yes, it can dampen your writing style because it makes it sound awkward and out of sync.

For example, faulty parallelism sometimes happens if you're using gerund phrases and then suddenly switch to infinitive phrases (*to* plus the main verb form).

Here's a sentence that shows faulty parallelism using gerund phrases used as an object, paired with an infinitive phrase:

On weekends we like going to parties, playing sports, and to see friends.

The last part of the sentence, *to see friends*, doesn't click grammatically with the rest of the sentence because the two other activities, going to parties and playing sports, have verbs ending in *ing*. To correct the sentence all you have to do is eliminate the *to* and tack an *ing* ending on *see*.

On weekends we spend time going to parties, playing sports, and seeing friends.

Here's another sentence using faulty parallelism:

Twisting, shouting, and to dance the night away keep me busy on summer nights.

If you want to make this sentence balanced and parallel, change *to dance* to *dancing* so that it sounds like the other verb endings:

Twisting, shouting, and dancing the night away keep my busy on summer nights.

You'll notice that I didn't use fancy grammatical terminology, such as *gerund phrase*, to analyze the last sentence. That's because I wanted you to see how you can look at a sentence intuitively, figure out the problem, and correct it.

While it helps to know the reasons behind why a sentence is written incorrectly, you can often figure it out without going into complicated explanations. After all, that's what you'll have to do if you're writing under pressure. You won't have time to mull over the piddling points of grammar. You'll have to depend on your best judgment to steer you right. And you can usually trust that.

Here's another example of faulty parallelism:

Incorrect Sentence: The CEO promised five paid sick days and that the cafeteria would offer pizza and pasta instead of beef hash and sardine salad.

Corrected sentence: The CEO promised *that we would get five paid sick days* **and** *that the cafeteria would offer pizza and pasta instead of beef hash and sardine salad.* (Two dependent clauses beginning with *that* solved the faulty parallelism problem.)

Faulty parallelism can also come into play when you compare or contrast ideas:

Example: Jonah liked learning languages more than to solve mathematical problems.

Correction: Jonah liked learning languages more than solving mathematical problems.

QUICK QUIZ #15: FAULTY PARALLELISM

Here's a quick quiz about parallel construction. This one has only five questions, so score 20 points for each correct answer. Rewrite each sentence to correct the error in faulty parallelism.

1. Melissa likes bowling, playing football, and to swim.
2. The dating service offers six months free and that you can renew at no cost if you can't find a suitable match.
3. To learn grammar is as important to good writing as having creative ideas.
4. Deepak praised his teacher for her understanding, ability to explain difficult concepts, and showing infinite patience.
5. Grace enjoys studying music more than to solve math problems.

THE SECOND PERSON

One more question. What's wrong with using *you* in writing? I always use it to make my writing sound more personal and friendly. My teacher says that every time she reads my essays she feels like I'm giving her a sermon.

When someone writes in the second person, *you*, it can sound preachy, making it seem that you're telling the reader what to do. Look at this example from a student's test paper and see how a reader might react to its tone:

You can learn a lesson from Macbeth. It's important to learn to make your own decisions and not to be so easily influenced because it might cause you trouble.

Now I see what you mean. How can I rewrite this to make it sound better?

You can easily correct this example by using the first person, *we* or *us*, or the third person (*one*, *the reader*, *people*, *they*, or *them*, for example). Look at the examples below and compare them to the one using the second person.

First person (*we*, *us*): By reading Macbeth *we* can learn the importance of making our own decisions and of not being swayed by others, which can lead *us* into difficult situations.

Third person (*readers*, *them*): By studying Macbeth, *readers* can learn the importance of making their own decisions and not being swayed by others, which can lead *them* into difficult situations.

You mentioned using *one*, the third person, instead of using second person, *you*. Doesn't that sound stuffy and pompous?

It depends on the situation. Think about your subject matter, and it will help you decide which person is best to use.

Compare these two sentences:

Formal topic (third person, *one*): Medical research has proven that one must avoid consuming excessive salt in order to lower blood pressure.

Informal topic (third person, *people*, *they*): People often shop on the weekends because they have more free time.

The bottom line in determining whether to use *one* or another third-person substitute relates to the tone of your message. If you want to figure out which tone to use, pretend you're talking to someone and say the sentence aloud.

If you believe that how you're saying it would help you reach your target audience the way you want it to, go with your instincts. Keep your audience in mind at all times when you're speaking and writing, and ask yourself which words would best help them get your message and take away something from it. Ask yourself how you can best connect with your reader.

QUICK QUIZ #16: FINE-TUNING YOUR WRITING STYLE

Now that we've talked about some language pitfalls to avoid if you want your writing style to sound fresh and original, it's time for your last quiz. Errors include deadwood, clichés, nonstandard English, jargon, euphemisms, slang, ending a sentence with a preposition, and the second person.

Experiment with the sentences until you find the right mix of words to correct the error. Write the name of the error to the left of your corrections. Although your wording may be different from that in the answer key, it may still be correct if you've eliminated the error. Use your best judgment in scoring. Give yourself 5 points for naming the error and 5 points for the correction.

1. _____ After the doctor said to apply the paddles stat, the patient's heartbeat returned to normal.

2. _____ The boss told Cassandra that she'd be let go from her job if she didn't reach her sales quota.

3. _____ "I'm going to get the homework off Shawn because I'm too beat to do it," said Randy, not realizing that the teacher had overheard him.

4. _____ It's important to ponder all the implications of your deeds before embarking on a course of action.

5. _____ Ryleigh's visit from the stork left her with two six-pound twins.

6. _____ The early bird catches the worm, so I woke up at the crack of dawn.

7. _____ "You Ain't Nothin' But a Hound Dog," reached the top of the charts in the '50s.

8. _____ When my friend didn't meet me at the coffee shop, I wondered where she was at.

9. _____ If you want to make a good impression on an interview, you should not show up in jeans and a band shirt.

10. _____ The boss said that before we launch our advertising campaign to promote the new housing development, we'll have to get all our ducks in a row.

Chapter Twelve

How to Write Under Pressure
Using a Foolproof Plan

Does facing an essay exam send shock waves through your body? Does your brain freeze at the thought of recalling a semester's work and streamlining it into an essay that tells your teacher you're on top of the subject?

Don't panic. If you follow these easy steps, you'll never hesitate when you have to write an essay on any subject, whether it's a homework assignment, timed essay test, or placement exam.

If you're writing a business report, you can use the same five-step system to write reports that will impress your employer and possibly gain you a promotion.

What's the best way to prepare for an essay test? There's so much information to process. I don't know where to begin, so I get frustrated and usually end up cramming the night before. Then I don't remember anything I studied.

Coupled with planned study sessions (about an hour or two each night for a week or so before the test), this system will make your grades skyrocket. Rather than cramming, set aside a few nights for your review, and go over your teacher's notes and your textbook over a period of a few days. You can divide the material you need to learn into a few sessions, or you can give extra time to more difficult information and less to what comes easily to you. Be creative and do what's best for you, given your learning style and time limitations.

Think of how you work best. Some students choose to sit at a desk with a straight-back chair; others prefer to sit on the floor with their books sprawled out; and others like to use the kitchen table. Maybe you need absolute quiet, so you head off to the library. Some students enjoy playing music while they study. Contrary to what you've heard, there is no right or wrong way to study. What's most comfortable for you works best.

Once you've found your ideal system to study, gather your class notes, your textbook, and a pen and pad or a notebook. Avoid loose papers because recording the material you're studying in one space (a notebook or loose-leaf book) will help you organize your thoughts better. Highlighters in different colors work well for underlining important points as you jot down review notes.

FOCUS YOUR STUDY

Now that I've organized everything, where do I begin? Sometimes there's so much to learn, it overwhelms me.

Open up a fresh notebook when you start your review sessions. You may want to keep one for each subject, accumulating review notes you can go back to for all your tests, including midterms and finals.

Using your class notes as a guideline for what you think you'll be tested on, look at the chapter headings in your textbook, and under each heading jot down the main points from your notes and the text.

Be sure to give extra attention to material your teacher said you'd need to know for the test and to any information the teacher said to remember or made a point of repeating. Use highlighters, asterisks, or underlining to emphasize main points.

It's important before the test to convince your teacher to give you some idea of how to focus your study. If the teacher doesn't volunteer information, you be the one to ask. Use your persuasive powers to get the teacher to be specific. Find out what material the test will cover and what type of test it is: essay, multiple choice, or a combination.

If you have a teacher who won't review, talk to students who have had that teacher before to get an idea of what types of things to study. You'll probably already have an idea of what's going to be on the test when you look over your notes to see what the teacher stressed in class.

Save time: use abbreviations when taking notes on your textbook. Use your own shorthand. Nobody else has to understand it, but make sure you remember your secret codes. Make your writing legible enough so that you can read it. Using a computer will help ensure that.

Repeat important points aloud to yourself as you record them. If you write the main points and read what you're writing aloud, you'll recall the material better. The more senses you use in learning, the better your mind will retain the information. Always **Read**, **Write**, and **Say It Aloud** to recall whatever you need to learn.

THE FIVE-STEP PLAN

Once you've spent a few days mastering the material, it's time to put your writing plan into action. The five steps to writing a perfect essay or report are: **brainstorm, organize, write, proofread,** and **revise**—in that order. If you leave out any of the steps, the system won't be as effective. Whether you're a student aiming to ace an essay test or a professional who wants to write topnotch reports, make it a point to follow the five- step plan.

If you're writing an essay or business report in a pressured situation, it's important to wear your watch. If you time each stage of the writing process, you'll be able to complete your writing task with ease and even have time left to proofread and revise to perfection.

Brainstorm

I've tried outlining, but when I do, I never have time to finish my essay and forget about proofreading and revising. I'm lucky if I get all the answers down before the time's up.

You have to trust that this system I'm giving you for acing essays will work. That's the first step. Then you have to muster the courage to try it in a real testing situation. You've come this far. You've learned about sentence structure, grammar, punctuation, and writing style. Now it's time to put it all together and to use it to your advantage.

Maybe you've experienced something like this. You're ten minutes into the test, and you see the students around you writing furiously. You notice that one student has run up to the teacher's desk for more paper (if you're in college, another blue book).

And there you sit, still juggling your outline with only thirty minutes left in the period. Sure, it's scary, but this anxiety, if you experience it at all, will pass after your first time trying this system because you'll find it makes the difference between an average grade and a top grade.

The first thing to do when you get your test is to **read each question carefully.** Does the question ask you to list, compare, contrast, analyze, or discuss? Be sure to do exactly what you're asked. Then on a piece of scrap paper or the cover of the blue book, begin to list in a few words or phrases (not sentences—there isn't enough time) your best ideas for answering the question.

Since you're pressed for time, don't worry about composing a formal outline with Roman numerals and capital letters. That's not important when you're racing against the clock.

When you brainstorm, you're throwing out ideas you think might answer the question. Don't be afraid to take a chance. List any ideas that come to mind. You can always scrap them later.

Write your ideas in list form. For each essay you'll want to write three to eight main points, depending on the detail the question requires. Under the main points you can list two or three supporting details. Use either words or brief phrases, whatever you think will best help you remember how to flesh out your essay when you're ready to write.

To simplify your task, you may want to list only the main points and then fill in the details when you write your essay. Do what's best for you. Let the content of the question guide you on how much material you need to cover.

Think of this stage of writing your essay as a brainstorming session, a rapid-fire one. Depending on how many questions there are, allow no more than five or ten minutes for this phase of essay writing. Devote most of your time to the actual writing. This is one time you'll want to be a clock watcher.

Organize

When you complete your brief outline, look it over and see if there's anything you need to add or omit. Then arrange the outline in a logical order by numbering the topics in order of their importance. (Don't bother to rewrite your outline. Just juggle those numbers in front of your topics to give your essay a sense of organization.)

If you take the time to outline before you write, you'll cover the most important points and won't be tempted to pad your essay or business report with irrelevant facts.

How will this brief outline help me when I write?

Now that you've completed your outline, you'll write an answer that's based on the question, one that your teacher is looking for. You'll feel much more confident than you would if you had started writing without first organizing. Then you'd be tempted to go off the subject and stray from the most important ideas you intended to cover.

Write

I hear what you're saying, but I also need help with how to actually begin writing my essay. Where do I start when the pressure's on?

All you have to do is write a topic sentence that takes into account the question and possibly repeats part of the question. After you do this, give an idea in your topic sentence of how you intend to answer the question. This gives your teacher a roadmap for knowing what will come next and will show that you have a good sense of organization.

As an example, here's a question for an English exam on poetry: "Discuss how the sonnet form in Elizabeth Barrett Browning's poem 'How Do I Love Thee?' contributes to the poem's meaning."

Your first sentence might read: "In Elizabeth Barrett Browning's poem, the tight sonnet form contributes to the poem's meaning by adding discipline and restraint to a highly emotional topic." You've stated the question and immediately given an idea of the approach you'll use in answering the question.

When I begin to write, what's a good way to bring my ideas together so that the essay or report makes sense?

Now that you've brainstormed, outlined, and organized your ideas, it's time to write. Your job will be easy because your outline will guide you in answering the question. Be sure to use transitions to tie your thoughts together and to bridge the gaps between paragraphs. (We talked about transitions, also called parenthetical expressions, in Chapter Six, when we discussed commas.)

We said that words like *also, in addition to this, additionally, since, however, on the other hand,* and *in conclusion* can prepare the reader for what lies ahead and can make your essay pleasurable to read instead of a chore because it's well-organized and easy to follow. As you know, teachers reward writing that's pleasurable to read with a good grade. Similarly, businesses often promote people who can represent the company in a positive light by communicating clearly.

As you write, keep an eye on your outline so that you don't stray from the main points and drift off into side issues. When you come to the end of your essay or report, you'll want to bring it to a smooth close. Restating your main idea and adding a new twist to what you said before presents a foolproof way for writing an effective ending to your essay.

As an ending sentence for our sample poetry essay, you might write something like this: "By using the sonnet form, Browning's poem has captured the emotions of eternal love without falling into the trap of sentimentality."

Proofread

Now that I've finally finished writing, there's not much time left to proofread. Is there a way I can do this quickly so that I can catch most of my mistakes?

You've composed your outline, organized your ideas, and followed the outline to write a memorable essay or report. Be sure to keep an eye on your watch. You'll need at least five minutes to proofread and revise your essay. Quickly scan your paper to make sure that everything makes sense. Even the best writer can easily leave out a word or use the wrong word, causing an essay to look unpolished and unprofessional.

Revise

Next, search for spelling mistakes, run-on sentences, and fragments. These three errors will jump-start your teacher's red pen and drastically lower your grade. If you're not sure of how to spell a word, substitute a synonym you know how to spell. If you have time and aren't in a pressured writing situation, you can consult an electronic spell check or a dictionary.

However, use caution when using your computer's spelling or grammar check as it may create errors far worse than your original error. If you want to use this electronic genie (notice I didn't say *genius*), look at the proposed correction and use your best judgment in applying it.

If you see a run-on sentence, try correcting it by adding punctuation (period or semicolon) or a conjunction (*and* or *but*). You can easily correct a sentence fragment by adding more words. If a sentence doesn't make sense, it won't work.

If you have extra time, check to see that you've added transitions between paragraphs, and neatly cross out anything you think will sabotage your essay's success. It's important that your teacher or employer can read your handwriting, so make your final copy as neat as possible and large enough to read.

Another thing to think about as you write your revision is the use of contractions. You've probably noticed that I use contractions freely throughout this book—that's because I wanted you to feel that I was talking to you directly. When we converse with people, we talk in a more relaxed, casual manner.

If you're writing a formal paper, you'll use a more formal tone. Think about how contractions and your choice of wording can make your reader receive an entirely different message than one in which you avoided contractions and employed a more sophisticated vocabulary.

Ask yourself what your writing goals are for each project before you write or revise. If you're writing for a general audience, you may want to choose words that everyone will readily grasp and to use more contractions to add a more reader-friendly essay or report. However, if you're writing a scholarly piece or a formal report, you'll want to take it up a notch, eliminating slang or casual wording and avoiding contractions.

You'll also want to consider paragraphing when you revise. Most teachers and employers like to read writing that's easy on the eyes. You can grant them their wish by writing one idea to a paragraph. Try not to make your paragraphs longer than eight or nine lines. Readers respond better to short paragraphs. Use transitions (linking words) within and between paragraphs to give your readers clues about what will follow.

Ready to Write

You've learned the right amount of grammar to help you write better. Punctuation's easy for you now. You've followed the five steps to successful essay and report writing: brainstorm, organize, write, proofread, and revise. Now you're ready to write.

Never again will you hear your teacher or employer proclaim: "Excuse me, your participle's dangling!" because now you're completely confident about your grammar skills. You're ready to make your writing powers soar!

Answer Key

Note to the reader: If you decided to peek at the answer key, stop right here. Try the sentences yourself first, and then if you had trouble with any of the questions, go back and figure out where you went wrong.

QUICK QUIZ #1: ACTION VERB OR LINKING VERB?

1. L: *Felt* deals with feelings, not action.
2. A: You can picture Tasha tasting the spiders.
3. A: The troll actively did something.
4. L: The casserole didn't actively do anything; it just tasted that way.
5. A: Picture Antoine's mother sounding an alarm. You can't get more active than that.
6. A: Dylan did something to win the contest. He made the plants grow, so *grew* is an action verb.
7. L: You can substitute *was* for *sounded*, and nothing is happening.
8. A: Bongo smelled the salmon and did flips.
9. A: Visualize Andrew listening to the horse's heartbeat.
10. L: You can substitute *was*. Also, you can't see any action.

QUICK QUIZ #2: ACTIVE OR PASSIVE VOICE?

Explanation: It's easy to tell the difference between active voice and passive voice. Active voice is pure action without the excess words. Passive voice consists of the past participle of the main verb plus part of the verb *to be*.

1. P
2. A
3. P
4. A
5. A
6. P
7. A
8. A
9. P
10. A

QUICK QUIZ #3: SUBJECTS AND PREDICATES

To find the subject, you looked for the action word. You asked *who* or *what* in front of the predicate.

1. S: cat; P: ate
2. S: walrus; P: waddled
3. S: player; P: dunked
4. S: canary; P: existed
5. S: man; P: is

QUICK QUIZ #4: SENTENCE TYPES

1. C: This sentence has two subjects, *Lionel* and *nobody*, and two predicates, *grew* and *recognized*.
2. S: This sentence has one subject, *Esai*, and a compound predicate, *played* and *danced*.
3. C: This sentence has two subjects, *José* and *jellyfish* and two predicates, *jumped* and *grabbed*.
4. CX: The sentence has one independent clause: *A coworker saw her go into the local spa.* You'll also find one dependent clause here: *When Sandra took a day off from work.*
5. CC: This sentence has one dependent clause: *After Ben threw the lobster into the boiling water.* It has two independent clauses: *It leapt out of the pot* and *it chased him around the room.*
6. S: The sentence starts with a prepositional phrase, *at the bachelor party*, and is followed by an independent clause with a compound predicate, *A gigantic groundhog jumped out of the cake and fell into Hector's arms.*

7. CC: This sentence starts with a dependent clause: *Before she sat down in her chair.* It is followed by two independent clauses: *Ms. Priswell examined it for thumbtacks* and *instead she found a gift certificate from the class.*

8. CC: This sentence starts with a dependent clause: *After Melissa moved to a deserted farmhouse.* It is followed by two independent clauses: *She bought a pit bull for protection* and *she adopted a cat to kill the mice lurking in her attic.*

9. CC: There are two independent clauses in this sentence with two subjects, *girl* and *she*, and two predicates, *told* and *grew. That her bearded dragon lizard demolished her homework* is a dependent clause.

10. S: *gives* and *brings* are the compound predicates in this simple sentence.

QUICK QUIZ #5: WRITING DIFFERENT TYPES OF SENTENCES

Examples of Different Sentence Types

Simple Sentence: Drew won the tennis championship. (one independent clause)

Compound Sentence: Luke was awarded a baseball scholarship, and he received an offer from a pro team. (two independent clauses)

Complex Sentence: Cole received an offer from the Phillies because he played baseball passionately. (one independent and one dependent clause)

Compound-Complex Sentence: Theresa became a sportscaster, and she covered the NBA playoffs after she excelled in many college games. (two independent clauses and one dependent clause)

QUICK QUIZ #6: SENTENCE FRAGMENTS AND RUN-ON SENTENCES

1. SF: The second group of words is a fragment. It doesn't make sense by itself. It also begins with *that*, a relative pronoun, which tells you that a dependent clause is coming.

2. RO: This run-on uses a comma, rather than a period, to separate the two complete thoughts.

3. CS: This complex sentence is a complete sentence.

4. RO: This run-on contains two complete thoughts without using a period, semi-colon, or conjunction.

5. SF: This sentence is not a complete thought because it doesn't make sense; it also doesn't contain a predicate.

6. RO: The comma after *burps* makes this a run-on. It needs a period, semi-colon, or conjunction.

7. SF: The first group of words is a fragment because it isn't a complete thought; it's a dependent clause.

8. CS: This is a complete sentence that contains both an independent and a dependent clause.

9. RO: This is a run-on because there is no punctuation, such as a period, semicolon, or conjunction after *boss*.

10. CS: This is a complete sentence with two independent clauses joined by the conjunction *but*.

QUICK QUIZ #7: DANGLING AND MISPLACED MODIFIERS

1. MM: From my teacher I borrowed a book that contained pages of mind-deadening grammar exercises.

2. DM: After we studied all night, our eyes drooped the next morning; or, Our eyes drooped the morning after we studied all night.

3. DM: As I looked out the window, a purple-haired clown on stilts caught my eye.

4. DM: While riding a skateboard, Marisol was stung by a bee.

5. Sentence #1: The dog only howled. It didn't do anything else.
   Sentence #2: The only time the dog howled was when I was sleeping.

6. MM: John saw a parking ticket attached to his backpack.

7. MM: Juliet's roses were delivered in a porcelain vase by the florist; or, The florist delivered Juliet's roses in a porcelain vase.

8. DM: While I walked on the beach, a jellyfish stung my big toe.

9. DM: My mother gave me a silver scooter when I was six; or, When I was six, my mother gave me a silver scooter.

10. MM: There was a rose bush that smelled very fragrant next to the septic tank; or, Next to the septic tank, there was a rose bush that smelled very fragrant.

QUICK QUIZ: #8: COMMAS

1. I: yes,
   CC: desk,
2. DC: pet,
3. NC
4. Prep P: mountains,
5. AP: Malarkey, tales,

CS: died, failed, (If you left out the comma after *failed*, you can still give yourself credit.)

6. PE: opinion,
7. DC: me,
    D and A: 767 Road, Philadelphia,
8. NC
9. DA: "Jayden,
10. CC: too,
11. CS: cheeseburgers, fries, (If you left out the comma after *fries*, you can still get credit.)
    CC: milkshake,
12. NC
13. D and A: Avenue, Naples,
14. AP: Mabel, friend,
    CC: eighty,
15. NC

QUICK QUIZ #9 RESTRICTIVE AND NONRESTRICTIVE CLAUSES AND PHRASES

1. NR (students, school): The main point of the sentence relates to what the students planned to do. The fact that they anticipated a day off from school is added information.
2. NR (boss, chair): The fact that the boss fell is the main point of the sentence.
3. R: The clause *who cut class excessively* restricts the meaning of the sentence.
4. NR (Pablo, correctly): The clause that begins with the relative pronoun *who* is added information.
5. NR (Leah, loudly): The fact that Leah woke up her roommates is the main idea in the sentence.
6. R: Whenever you see a clause beginning with *that*, it's restrictive. Also, this clause is important because it refers specifically to these orders.
7. R: The clause beginning with *who* is restrictive because the teacher rewarded only those students who got an A.
8. NR (restaurant, Parsippany): The information about the restaurant's location provides additional information.
9. NR (ring, partners): The phrase beginning with *engraved* is added information that doesn't affect the meaning here.
10. R: The clause beginning with *who* is important as these people are the only ones required to attend the class.

QUICK QUIZ #10: THE REST OF THE PUNCTUATION MARKS

1. S: counselor;
2. A: managers'
3. I: *ah hum*
4. I: the *New York Times* (Do not italicize *the*.)
5. D or P:—the decision still amazes me—; or (the decision still amazes me)
6. C: students:
   S: studies; day; (Use a semicolon because the items in the series have commas. The items are also long, and the semicolons help us understand the sentence better.)
7. QO: "You're . . . test"? The question mark goes outside the quotes because the entire sentence is a question.
8. C
9. COM and IQ: said, "it . . . shows." Interrupted quote. Start with a small *i* for *it* after *said*. Put quotes before *it* and after *shows*.
10. QNS: "Today . . . movie," Mr. Lee said.
    "You . . . afternoon." The word *you* starts a new sentence.

QUICK QUIZ #11: AGREEMENT

1. are: Use plural because you have a compound subject joined by *and*.
2. is: *Tossing and turning* is thought of as one thing.
3. C: *Everyone* is considered singular, so use a singular verb.
4. has: Use a singular verb with a compound subject joined by *or*.
5. has: *Knowledge* is a singular subject. Use a singular verb.
6. was: *Fruit* is considered one thing, so use a singular verb.
7. are: The second subject, *counselors,* is plural. Use the plural verb *are*.
8. C: *One* is considered singular, so use a singular verb.
9. like: *None* is considered plural here, so use a plural verb.
10. is: *Hot dogs and baked beans* is considered one thing, so use *is*, a singular verb.

QUICK QUIZ #12: USING INCLUSIVE LANGUAGE

1. There are a number of ways to correct this sentence. Here are two: You can make the sentence plural: *Students* packed a lunch for *their* trip to the zoo. You could also eliminate *his*. Each student packed a lunch for the trip to the zoo.
2. Eliminate *her*: *Everyone in the office pooled resources* . . .
3. Use *mail carrier* instead of *mailman.*

4. Make everything plural. *Employees* will receive a bonus if *they* reach a high quota in computer sales.
5. Change *firemen* to *firefighters.*

QUICK QUIZ #13: PRONOUNS

1. him and me: Use the object pronouns *him* and *me* with the object of the preposition *for.*
2. C: than he gave me
3. C: than I am
4. her, me: Use objective case pronouns as they're the objects of the predicate *told.*
5. Andy and me: *Andy* and *me* are the objects of the preposition *for.*
6. I: Eliminate *It was me.* Instead, you could say: I called you at 3:00 a.m. to ask if you had anything good in your house to eat. If you want to sound more formal, and maybe a little uppity, you could say *It was I.*
7. C: It's correct because *me* is the indirect object of *gave.*
8. I: Use *I* because, along with *coworker*, it's the subject of the sentence.
9. me: *Me* is correct because it's the object of the verb *helps.*
10. C: The sentence is correct: *My friend and I* are in the nominative case because of the linking verb *were.*

QUICK QUIZ #14: WORDS OFTEN CONFUSED

1. b: Since they did it before you got there, use *already.*
2. a: *Affected* is the only verb to use here.
3. a: The only correct form of the word is *all right*—two words.
4. b: Use *altogether*, meaning completely.
5. a: *A lot* (two words) is the only way to spell the word.
6. a: The right answer is *illusion*, which means a trick. An *allusion* is a reference to something.
7. b: *Apprised* is the only choice here because it means to let her know. *Appraise* is to assess the worth of something.
8. b: *A while* is correct because it means an amount of time that's undetermined. *Awhile* means for a time.
9. a: *Coarse* is correct because it means crude. *Course* means a path of action or travel, or something you take in school.
10. b: *Complemented* means looks good with, while *complimented* means telling someone you liked something about them.
11. b: *Uninterested* means that Milo doesn't like science. *Disinterested* means that a person is impartial.

12. a: *Ingenuous* means that Sofia seemed innocent. *Ingenious* means clever or skillful.

13. b: *Its* is correct because it shows possession, while *it's* is the contraction for it is.

14. a: *Fewer* is right because it refers to a specific number, while *less* refers to an unspecific number.

15. b: *Lay* is the past tense of lie (to rest or lie down), while *laid* is the past tense of lay, to put down an object.

16. b: *Laid* is right because laid is the past tense of lay, to put down.

17. b: *Principles* are values, and *principals* are school leaders. *Principal* can also mean the most important.

18. a: *They're* is a contraction for *they are*, while *their* is a possessive pronoun meaning ownership.

19. a: *That* is the answer because you need it to begin a restrictive clause, one that's important to the sentence.

20. b: Use *fewer* because it's a countable amount.

QUICK QUIZ #15: FAULTY PARALLELISM

1. Melissa likes bowling, playing football, and swimming; or, Melissa likes to bowl, to play football, and to swim.
2. The dating service offers six months free and renewal at no cost.
3. Learning grammar is as important to good writing as having creative ideas.
4. Deepak praised his teacher for her understanding, ability to explain difficult concepts, and infinite patience.
5. Grace enjoys studying music more than solving math problems.

QUICK QUIZ #16: FINE-TUNING YOUR WRITING STYLE

1. **jargon**: After the doctor said to apply the paddles immediately, the patient's heartbeat returned to normal. (*Stat* is medical jargon, meaning *immediately*.)
2. **euphemism**: The boss told Cassandra that she'd be fired if she didn't reach her sales quota. *Let go* is a euphemism for fired.
3. **slang**: "I'm going to *copy the homework* from Sean because I'm *too tired* to do it," said Randy, not realizing that the teacher had overheard him.
4. **deadwood**: It's important to think about the consequences of your actions before you decide what to do. (The original sentence rambles on.)
5. **euphemism**: Ryleigh *delivered* (or gave birth to) two six-pound twins.

6. **clichés**: The person who takes time to plan ahead will succeed, so I woke up early.

7. **nonstandard English**: Change to: "You aren't anything but a hound dog." "You ain't nothin'" is nonstandard English. Since the song grossed a lot of money back in the '50s, most people probably would not care about its title. However, this song title is a good example of nonstandard English, which is the worst kind you can use.

8. **ending a sentence with a preposition**: When my friend didn't meet me at the coffee shop, I wondered where she was. (In this case, we simply eliminated the preposition *at*.)

9. **second person**: If a person (or someone) wants to make a good impression on an interview, he (or she) shouldn't show up in jeans and a band shirt. You don't have to write the words that you see in parentheses. They're there to give you alternatives. If you want to use inclusive language, you could also make the entire sentence plural. Most people would probably agree that this would sound better.

10. **jargon:** The boss said that before we launch our advertising campaign to promote the new housing development, we'll have to organize and plan the details of the campaign carefully. (*Get all our ducks in a row* is jargon people in the business world often use.)

About the Author

Catherine DePino has written many books for children, teachers, and parents about writing improvement and bully prevention. She also wrote two upbeat nondenominational prayer books for teenagers. She holds a doctorate from Temple University and served for many years as an English teacher and department head of English, world languages, and ESL in Philadelphia schools. Additionally, she worked for Temple as a student teaching supervisor.